D0375815

CROSSING
BOUNDARIES

Praise for *Crossing Boundaries*

"Aziz Abu Sarah articulates something I have long believed about travel: that it has the potential to help heal and regenerate the planet not just by protecting nature and cultures but also by promoting understanding and peace. And he rightly reminds us that it's not more travel we should be after but the right kind of travel—one that treads lightly, highlights multiple perspectives (including traditionally marginalized ones), and fosters personal transformation, which is the key to a better world."
—Norie Quintos, independent tourism consultant and Editor at Large, National Geographic Travel Media

"*Crossing Boundaries* reminds us that travel at its best is so much more than selfies and Instagram moments. It is breaking bread and sharing exotic flavors, powerful conversations, and transformational experiences with strangers who quickly become friends and sometimes even family. Whether we're on a trip across town or an expedition halfway around the world . . . history, art, food, religion, and politics mean very little without human connection and real conversation. Aziz Abu Sarah is a guide in the truest sense of the word, ushering in the powerful new age of experiential travel. Read *Crossing Boundaries* and get off the beaten path to discover your own humanity. Let the adventure begin."
—Mark Bauman, former Senior Vice President, Smithsonian Media

"*Crossing Boundaries* is essential reading for any budding traveler. For an inexperienced traveler, it's a great handbook of how to navigate your way around the world—from avoiding overtourism hotspots to ensuring you are meeting and interacting with local people during your journey. For an experienced traveler, there are lots of important reminders about traveling safely, but more importantly, this book encourages you to reassess your travel style, your attitudes, and your behavior.

"I really enjoyed Aziz's book as it reflects Intrepid's vision, which is to change the way people see the world. Travel is vital to cultural understanding and can go a long way toward limiting conflict and war all over the world."
—Geoff Manchester, cofounder and Director, Intrepid Travel

"Brimming with humor and humanity, Aziz Abu Sarah is a perfect tour guide. His philosophy of travel penetrates deeply into intriguing places and unknown cultures, but more importantly, he plumbs the warm and vital depths of the human heart. In this book, you can go there with him without ever leaving home."

—**Geraldine Brooks, winner of the Pulitzer Prize in Fiction for** *March*

"Long before 'responsible travel' became a buzzword, Aziz was showing the world what it was. He is a true diplomat for world travel in the very best sense of the word. One of my fondest travel memories was dinner at his home on the West Bank with our Palestinian and Israeli guides. He showed us not only how to travel well but how to find a wonderful common ground in one of the most divided regions of our world. I hope all travelers read this book."

—**Jean Newman Glock, travel writer, Top Ten Worldwide Travel Expert (Klout), and CEO, JNG Worldwide**

CROSSING BOUNDARIES

A Traveler's Guide to
WORLD PEACE

AZIZ ABU SARAH

Berrett–Koehler Publishers, Inc.

Copyright © 2020 by Aziz Abu Sarah

All rights reserved. No part of this publication may be reproduced, distributed, or transmitted in any form or by any means, including photocopying, record-ing, or other electronic or mechanical methods, without the prior written per-mission of the publisher, except in the case of brief quotations embodied in critical reviews and certain other noncommercial uses permitted by copyright law. For permission requests, write to the publisher, addressed "Attention: Permissions Coordinator" at the address below.

Berrett-Koehler Publishers, Inc.
1333 Broadway, Suite 1000
Oakland, CA 94612-1921
Tel: (510) 817-2277
Fax: (510) 817-2278
www.bkconnection.com

ORDERING INFORMATION

Quantity sales. Special discounts are available on quantity purchases by corporations, associations, and others. For details, contact the "Special Sales Department" at the Berrett-Koehler address above.

Individual sales. Berrett-Koehler publications are available through most bookstores. They can also be ordered directly from Berrett-Koehler: Tel: (800) 929-2929; Fax: (802) 864-7626; www.bkconnection.com.

Orders for college textbook / course adoption use. Please contact Berrett-Koehler: Tel: (800) 929-2929; Fax: (802) 864-7626.

Distributed to the U.S. trade and internationally by Penguin Random House Publisher Services.

Berrett-Koehler and the BK logo are registered trademarks of Berrett-Koehler Publishers, Inc.

Printed in the United States of America

Berrett-Koehler books are printed on long-lasting acid-free paper. When it is available, we choose paper that has been manufactured by environmentally responsible processes. These may include using trees grown in sustainable forests, incorporating recycled paper, minimizing chlorine in bleaching, or recycling the energy produced at the paper mill.

Library of Congress Cataloging-in-Publication Data

Names: Abu Sarah, Aziz, author.
Title: Crossing boundaries : a traveler's guide to world peace / Aziz Abu Sarah.
Description: Oakland, CA : Berrett-Koehler Publishers, [2020] I Includes bibliographical references and index.
Identifiers: LCCN 2020002022 I ISBN 9781523088553 (paperback) I ISBN 9781523088577 (epub) I ISBN 9781523088560 (pdf)
Subjects: LCSH: Tourism—Social aspects. I Peace—Religious aspects. I Travel—Social aspects.
Classification: LCC G156.5.S63 A28 2020 I DDC 306.4/819—dc23
LC record available at https://lccn.loc.gov/2020002022

First Edition

26 25 24 23 22 21 20   10 9 8 7 6 5 4 3 2 1

Cover design and interior illustration: Nola Burger
Book production and text design: Leigh McLellan Design
Copyeditor: Elissa Rabellino
Proofreader: Mary Hazlewood. *Indexer:* Ken Dellapenta

CONTENTS

CHAPTER 1

TRAVEL IS
A STATE OF MIND

THE FIRST TRIP you take feels the farthest.

When I was 18 years old, I had never traveled to a country outside the Middle East. I only spoke Arabic and some broken English. But despite my limited exposure to the world, I was confident in my knowledge of it. One day, however, I took what felt like the longest journey of my life: I traveled across town to study Hebrew in West Jerusalem.

I had visited the western side of Jerusalem before, but only as a dishwasher at an Israeli café. At the café, I didn't speak Hebrew, and no one really tried to speak to me. I didn't have any meaningful interactions with Israelis and never felt like I was treated as an equal.

For the Israelis, I was the Arab who washed the dishes, and that was as far as our relationship went. I worked and went home. I was just hoping to save money to buy a computer. But the job left me angry, convinced that I had nothing in common with Israelis.

When I started studying Hebrew, though, that trip from the east to the west of the city became more meaningful. It forced me to explore my own life through the other side. I remember one of the first days walking to my Hebrew class, when sounds of sirens suddenly cut across the skies.

The sirens—which you can hear across Israel on Holocaust Day and Memorial Day (for remembering Israelis killed in the Arab-Israeli conflicts)—caught me off guard. Suddenly, the crowds on Ben Yehuda Street stopped walking and stood still. This was typical for a moment of silence in Israel, but I had no knowledge of it.

I freaked out. I tried to ask people on the street what was going on, but they refused to talk—because they're not supposed to. I was always very into sci-fi books, so my brain went in bizarre directions, scrambling to find an explanation for their odd behavior. Were they being controlled by aliens? Were they robots?

I was less than a 20-minute walk from my house, and I felt like I had been dropped into a completely foreign environment and culture. Later, my Hebrew teacher took the time to explain these moments in which I had felt out of place. In retrospect, I wonder: What had all these Israelis thought, seeing me run around instead of standing still to commemorate the Holocaust? Did they think I was purposely being disrespectful? How much fear and hatred exist between our communities due to ignorance and fear?

I was fortunate in that the Hebrew class helped me overcome my fear and acclimate to this new and strange habitat down the street from me. I was the only Palestinian in the class, and it was the first time I had had any real interactions with Jews and Israelis as an equal. I was just another student in the classroom, and we all studied together. For the first time, I was learning about their culture and history. Our teacher had us listen to each other's music and discuss movies and television.

Although the class was just across town, going to and from it was an act of traveling, and it profoundly transformed me. Before, I had only seen Israelis as the ones who had killed my brother and shot at me on my way to school. I had never met everyday Israelis, who were just everyday people, living their lives just like me. And this journey occurred just a few minutes from my home. I faced my own ignorance—for example, I learned that not all Jews are Israelis and not all Israelis are Jews. I realized how little I knew, and I was excited to explore this new world.

Despite being born with no passport or citizenship, I've now traveled to more than 60 countries. As a cultural educator and peacemaker, I've worked in conflict zones and negotiated between enemy groups as part of my work at the Center for World Religions, Diplomacy, and Conflict Resolution in Arlington, Virginia. I've worked in Afghanistan with the Shia and Sunni communities, in Northern Ireland with Protestants and Catholics, and in South America with indigenous communities. I've established a socially responsible tour company (MEJDI Tours), a social enterprise that partners with local organizations to develop sustainable community tourism. And I've traveled around the world speaking and doing projects as a National Geographic Explorer and speaker for National Geographic Learning. But no trip has been as difficult as that first trip just down the street.

We can all experience self-transformation by traveling in our own neighborhoods. Travel is not about distance; sometimes it only requires walking across the street and learning about the people who live beside you. Perhaps this means visiting a neighbor who has different views or who speaks a different language. In Fairfax, Virginia (where I spend half of my year), 39.5 percent of residents speak a non-English language, and 14.4 percent are not US citizens; 50.6 percent are white, 19.3 percent are Asians, and 16.2 percent are Hispanic or Latino.[1]

Fairfax is not unique—such diversity exists in many cities around the world—but despite this diversity, there's a pervasive tendency toward insularity in our lives. We tend to stick to familiar social circles, spending time with those who look, think, or worship as we do. We'll travel and take photos of a secluded beach in Thailand (and post the photos on our social media to evoke the jealousy of friends, coworkers, and strangers) but come home without having spent any time with or learned about the lives of the Thai and Lao peoples. Even in our own neighborhoods, how much do we know about the stories and histories of our own communities? In other words, travel can begin at home, with a change of mind-set: a move from insularity and routine to a curiosity about the people around us.

From Fear to Transformation

When I was growing up, the barriers to meeting Israelis were complex, and the Israeli military occupation and the decades-long conflict dominated my views concerning the other half of the city.

For a Palestinian, even the simple act of driving could result in a life-threatening situation. One of my earliest memories was driving from my grandmother's house back to our family home in Bethany—at most a 10-minute drive—and running into an Israeli checkpoint.

Our car was pulled over by the army. The soldiers asked all of us to exit the vehicle. We obeyed, and they began searching all the men and boys—patting us down one by one. My middle brother, Fawzi, was stubborn when he was a teenager. And on this day, his stubbornness and the presence of an Israeli soldier was a bad combination.

One of the soldiers asked my brother to spread his legs. He complied. But the soldier shouted that it wasn't enough and kicked my brother between the legs to spread them farther apart. Fawzi got angry and gave the soldier a shove. In a split second, the soldier lifted his gun and pointed it at my brother, ready to shoot. As we shouted and cried, my father, along with the other soldiers, intervened to try to deescalate the situation.

My father demanded that my brother quiet down and behave. But Fawzi, consumed in his fury, wanted to fight. "He [the soldier] kicked me in my legs!" Fawzi shouted. My father replied, "Yeah, but he has a gun. He can shoot you."

I was terrified. This was my first real encounter with the Israeli Army. But cooler heads prevailed, and after additional security checks, we were allowed to pile back into the car and continue on our way. I remember my father's fury at Fawzi as we drove on to Bethany. My father is from an older generation; his cousin was killed during the Six-Day War, and in order to survive, he learned to keep his head down and not cause trouble. As a result, Fawzi was the target of a verbal tirade for the rest of the ride home, which involved a lot of the word "stupid!"

In the years ahead, my view of Israelis only worsened. When I was seven, I tried to give up on the idea of going to school. It was too dangerous, I concluded.

Prior to this decision, it had been a typical school day. I was watching the clock hands slowly spin around until the ringing of the bell, when I could grab my belongings and barge outside into the fresh air. However, on this day, a protest erupted outside. Instead of breathing in fresh air, I found myself choking on tear gas from canisters shot by Israeli soldiers.

I remember running to the bus stop, thinking I was going to suffocate. Arriving home with eyes still burning and crying from the gas, I told my mom very bluntly, "I don't want to go to school anymore. I could die. It's not worth it."

My mom insisted that it was not possible for my seven-year-old self to drop out, so she packed me an onion every day in my lunch bag—a local remedy to help with the tear gas.

After fourth grade, I was sent to the Dar al-Aytam school in the Old City, which was famous for being a battlefront. As a child, however, I was not aware of this. A few days in, a group of students pulled the sideburns of an ultra-orthodox Jewish man, and the Israeli Army raided the school.

The other students were used to this, so they knew how to escape quickly. I did not. As fully armed soldiers stormed into the school, everyone rushed into the halls and scattered. But by the time I figured out what was happening, I discovered that I was the only one left in the classroom. I was alone and terrified.

I felt stupid: how had I not thought about an escape route? This should have been the first thing to do when arriving at a new school, I told myself. Almost 30 years later, I still sometimes find myself looking for escape routes when I'm in confined places.

The event that shaped me the most, however, happened when I was nine. Just after dawn, Israeli soldiers stormed into our home. I remember the shouts, the terror, the interrogations. And then they took my 18-year-old brother, Tayseer, away. He was arrested for allegedly throwing stones at soldiers. I have memories of waking up early in the morning, stumbling onto a bus provided by the International Committee of the Red Cross, and waiting for hours before they released the prisoners into an open, fenced-off area. Families rushed toward the fencing while their imprisoned loved ones desperately searched for them from the other side of the fence.

When we finally noticed Tayseer behind the fence, our voices were drowned out by other families squeezed beside us, screaming over one another. The Israeli prison allowed us just 10 minutes for the visit. It was frantic and noisy, a frenzied competition for space—elbows flying, everyone hoping to have a rare moment with their loved one.

I was angry and frustrated. It was also summer, extremely hot, and no one gave us water. I remember one of the soldiers looked at me, and I looked into his eyes and thought he was evil. One thing was clear in my mind: he was, quite simply, the oppressor. This was the portrait I had of the Israelis: the soldiers who tore my family apart and managed the prison that kept my brother inside a cage.

Soon after, my brother was released from prison. But by then, his organs were failing from the beatings he had sustained during Israeli interrogation sessions. We rushed him to the hospital, but he died from his injuries.

By the time I turned 18, this was the world I knew: my brother had been tortured to death by the Israeli Army. My dad's cousin had been lynched at a gas station by Israeli extremists. And several of my fellow students in high school had been shot by the Israeli military at protests.

As I grew up, these realities enraged me. I became very active politically and joined the Fatah Youth Movement. I wrote articles for the Fatah youth magazine and demonstrated in protests.

But after graduating from high school and struggling to find a job, I realized that I had to learn Hebrew if I wanted to work or study. I signed up for a Hebrew course; it was time for me to make that dreaded trip to the other side.

Crossing that line to West Jerusalem remains, to this day, one of the hardest things I have ever done. Yet, it changed my life. I can't even imagine what my life would have become if I hadn't attended that Hebrew class.

Crossing Boundaries

We are often afraid to ask questions. At times, we feel it's more comfortable (and polite) not to ask. This creates a fake peace. We maintain a smile and claim to be working together. But what if we asked hard questions? What if we found ways to travel into one another's lives—that unknown country that holds all the risks and discomforts of relationship?

If there's anyone who has the right to be angry at the Israelis, it's my father. Owing to his past, he's also one of the least likely to cross to the other side.

My family lost most of their possessions during the 1948 Arab-Israeli War. My grandparents had raised livestock and owned a large farm in Jerusalem, and during the war, all of their animals either were killed or went missing.

My father, being the oldest, was forced to drop out of school and started working to help support his four brothers and sisters. He began selling fruit on the streets of the Old City. He ended up doing very well for himself, eventually owning his own business. He leased land in Jericho and sold bananas and watermelons across the West Bank; this expanded to exporting fruit to the rest of the Middle East.

In 1967, however, another war broke out. My father's brother had gone to work in Amman, Jordan; when he realized what was happening, he tried to return but found the border closed. He remained in Jordan and was not allowed to visit Jerusalem again until the Oslo Accords between the PLO and Israel were signed in 1993. My father's brother wasn't the only one: about half of my father's family ended up being displaced in Jordan.

Our family had been ripped apart, stranded on opposite sides of the Jordan River.

The border closed, my father's export business collapsed. He also learned that one of his cousins had died trying to escape the fighting. Another war had once again turned his life upside down. He had lost his education and livelihood; half of his family was displaced in another country; one day his cousin was alive and well, and the next morning she was draped under a white sheet. All of this had been due to the conflict with Israel. How much could one person possibly take?

My father is resilient. He tried to restart his life and attempted several businesses. Unfortunately, he was never able to recover financially. By the time I was born, my family could barely find enough money to send me to a good school.

For my father, the losses seemed to never end. His son Tayseer was killed. Then another cousin was murdered by Israelis. My father's cousin had been working at a gas station late at night. A car full of Israelis pulled up, and my father's cousin filled their tank with gas. But when it came time to pay for the gas, the young men grabbed his arm and slammed on the accelerator, dragging him across the pavement and down the street until he died.

You would expect my father to be reeling with hatred and anger. But incredibly, he wasn't. On the contrary, after each tragic death my father sat us down and warned us, "Don't do anything stupid. Do not get involved in revenge. That's not the way to solve this." He feared one of his young sons would grab a knife and go seek revenge on the Israelis.

Then, about 20 years ago, a friend of the family, Dr. Adel, told my father about the Bereaved Families Forum, an organization that brought together Israeli and Palestinian families who had lost sons and daughters, fathers and mothers, in the conflict.

Adel's father had been killed by an Israeli settler, and the doctor turned to this organization for reconciliation, justice, and peace.

My father and mother visited once out of respect for Dr. Adel. They weren't sure about joining, but they knew I was interested in the activities related to the conflict, so after attending, they asked if I might like to go to a meeting. I excitedly said, "Great. Will you come with me?" My father looked at me and gave a resounding "No. I went once. That was enough." He added, "You should go. But please be careful." My father was worried that I would say the wrong thing and get myself thrown in jail. To this day, my father is still terrified to talk about politics with me when I call.

I attended the meetings, and within a few years I became the chairman of the organization. Then one year, I persuaded my father to attend a conference we had organized, presenting the dual histories of Israelis and Palestinians side by side. I explained that I was speaking and it would mean a lot if he came. He was open to it but understandably pessimistic.

This conference was one of his first real meetings with Israelis. He listened to the lectures. At the end of one session, the mediator asked if anyone had questions. My father raised his hand and shouted "I do!"

Like any son, I hoped they would not call on him. I expected that whatever my father was about to say would be embarrassing. Even though he lived in the same city as Israelis, he had zero knowledge of them. It was the first time he had heard Israelis speak about their lives and experiences, alongside Palestinian speakers who did the same.

My father started with "So you mentioned this Holocaust thing . . ." My heart dropped in my chest; no one has ever started a sentence with that comment and followed it up with anything constructive. I never felt like I wanted to disappear from a place as much as in that moment. I slumped down a bit in my chair, hoping no one would notice me. My father continued, "This Holocaust thing, did it actually happen? Or is it just political manipulation used by the Israeli government?"

Silence gripped the room. The hall was filled with 200 to 300 Israelis and Palestinians, many of whom were experts in peace work. Still, no one wanted to tackle that question. Meanwhile, I was praying the earth would open up and swallow me whole—anything to escape the palpable tension in that room.

The truth is that many Palestinian participants had the same question but didn't have the audacity to ask it like my father. The Israelis also knew that we Palestinians have that question in our heads—always unanswered and quietly hovering in our thoughts.

After what seemed like an eternity of silence, someone finally spoke up. It was Rami Elhanan, whose daughter had been killed by a Palestinian suicide bomber in 1997 and whose father was a survivor of Auschwitz. Rami replied to my father, "You know what? It is absurd for us to expect you to believe in something you have never learned about."

He offered to take my father to the Holocaust Museum in Jerusalem. And my father accepted, and went. Not only did my father take up the opportunity; so did 70 other Palestinians—all of whom were bereaved parents. Rami's father and a few other Holocaust survivors led the tour through the museum, sharing their stories.

The Palestinian bereaved families asked hard questions. And they had a million of them. They were not used to Israelis, so they were unsure what was offensive and what wasn't. In the end, however, the trip went very well.

The museum visit taught us how powerful this kind of inter-cultural travel could be. As Israelis and Palestinians, we were all living next to one another but knew nothing about one another. So we began setting up tours for the members of our organization to learn about each other's histories.

Our idea was to find a way in which both sides would be able to travel into each other's lives. One week we would focus on personal histories of both sides. We discussed the Nakba (the Palestinian "catastrophe," which Israelis celebrate as Independence Day), when 750,000 Palestinians were displaced during Israel's creation in 1948. Palestinian elders who had lived through the event would host Israelis and tell their stories. Likewise, the Israelis would invite us to their homes so we could get a glimpse into their lives and histories.

It wasn't about comparing suffering. It was about crossing these lines that we had never crossed before. I can promise you that none of those Israelis or Palestinians who joined these tours had ever had a more meaningful and challenging travel experience in their lives. And more than 15 years later, this project is still alive and going strong: thousands of Israelis and Palestinians have participated in learning each other's narratives and histories.

One of the Israeli members of the Bereaved Families Forum, Sharon, once worked in the educational unit of the Israeli Army. Although she had never worked at checkpoints or served in combat, fear of Palestinians still shaped her life as an Israeli. The two of us decided to start hosting a radio show about the stories of Palestinians and Israelis.

One day, I invited her to my house in East Jerusalem. She agreed but was noticeably worried about the visit. She parked her car outside my house, close to the garbage bin, and hurried inside. About a half hour later, someone knocked on the door. It was a neighbor, who told me in Arabic to move the car because the garbage had caught fire; he and other neighbors were worried that our guest's car might get damaged. But Sharon, who does not speak Arabic, immediately thought someone had intentionally set her car on fire because they knew she was Israeli.

When I explained to her that the neighbors were only concerned about her car, she was surprised. It was a big deal for her: people she thought were out to get her were only coming to help. This made a huge impact on her, and she began coming to East Jerusalem more frequently and building connections with Palestinians.

It's an invaluable experience to get out of our comfort zone, visit an unfamiliar community, and hear narratives that conflict with our own. It's not an easy form of travel. But hearing others' stories does not need to negate our own identity and beliefs. It does force us to open our mind, however, to other realities—some of which exist just down the street.

Cultivating a Spirit of Exploration

Israel and Palestine are an extreme example, but I've seen these same processes occur in other places in the world. Let's take a trip to Washington, DC, where I lived part-time for several years. We wanted to organize a dual narrative tour to bring people to the historical Anacostia neighborhood, a predominantly poor black area. It has important sites, like the Frederick Douglass National Historic Site, and an assortment of black churches.

We started with a pilot trip and invited people in DC to participate. These were open-minded people: some described themselves as progressives. Yet none of them had visited their neighbors in Anacostia before.

We started at the Frederick Douglass National Historic Site and then visited a local church. We talked about the role of faith in social justice. We then took a trip to some other parts of the city that most of the group had never visited. We met with the Heritage Foundation, a conservative organization, to hear them talk about their vision for the city. We followed that up with a meeting with a councilman from one of the progressive neighborhoods in Washington, who talked about gentrification and its effect on underprivileged communities. Even as we visited some of the most popular sites in Washington, like the Lincoln Memorial and the Korean War Veterans Memorial, our discussions evolved into understanding the "other side."

The truth is, you can live in a city for a decade, but not truly get to know it. We tend to surround ourselves with people who look like us, who share our political views, and who worship like us. In this sense, Washington, DC, is not that different from Jerusalem. The dividing lines might not be as visible as in Jerusalem, but these borders are no less real.

I always wanted to explore Vietnam, for instance; I am in love with the country. But for years I ignored the fact that Washington, DC, has a huge Vietnamese community. Now I realize how ridiculous it was to travel all the way to Vietnam to listen to stories there while ignoring the Vietnamese community in my own city. I had also never reached out to the Indian community in my city, or the Ethiopian community—and these are the people who live beside me.

I'm a firm believer that if I don't explore or travel within my own community, then I'm not going to do it even if I travel 5,000 miles away. If I don't have a travel mind-set at home, traveling abroad will most likely result in my staying at a resort and seeing the go-to top-10 sites. But it's unlikely that I'll really learn about the people or put myself in situations in which I'll hear different perspectives or step outside of my comfort zone.

In other words, before traveling, we should ask ourselves a few questions: Have I reached out to people in my own community? What are the different cultures that exist in my own area? What are the different ethnic groups? What kinds of dif-

ferent foods are being cooked around me? And, most important, what stories, perspectives, and histories exist here? What
can I explore and learn in my own environment before I buy
a ticket to travel to a far-off part of the world? And if I am not
able to break boundaries and borders within my own community, how am I going to be able to do it when I travel outside my
country?

Traveling within our own city is not easy—but it is important for becoming more compassionate. Not every interaction I
had with an Israeli was positive. I've been called racial slurs by
16-year-old Israeli schoolchildren. I can't even count the number
of times I've had a face-palm moment, like being asked by Israelis
why I don't just get Israeli citizenship (when it's almost impossible for Jerusalem residents to become citizens), or being asked
why Palestinians in Jerusalem don't pay Israeli taxes (we pay the
same taxes they do). But even these interactions become learning
experiences. I also realize that many in my own community have
similar assumptions about Israelis that are incorrect.

I cannot be angry at those Israeli teens who called me a
"murderer"—because I used to be exactly like them. I cannot
judge those Israelis who ask ignorant questions, because they
quite literally do not know. I grew up believing that every Israeli
was a child killer, all of them hated us, and they all wanted to
expel us from the land. But the more I learned, the more I came
to understand that this was not true. And some of those same
Israeli schoolchildren who seemed driven by hatred ended up
apologizing an hour and a half later after hearing a different
perspective.

When dealing with conflict, we can choose to scoff at those
who don't know and treat them as bigots, or we can look at them
with compassion and understand that they haven't been given
the opportunity to learn.

Toward Transformative Travel

Travel does not just mean journeying abroad or escaping to a pristine beach paradise: travel can be anything that helps us explore people, cultures, and environments. Travel is about exploration. At times, this exploration can be challenging. But the most crucial travel we can experience is usually just outside our front door.

With that in mind, whether you are a new traveler hoping to make a difference and participate in a movement of social change or a seasoned traveler who has seen it all and is looking for ways to travel more responsibly, this book is a guide to a different kind of travel. It is a strategy book for how to have transformative, sustainable, and responsible travel experiences.

As such, the book is roughly divided into three sections. The first six chapters make the case for responsible travel, arguing why it is important to change our travel habits, and giving practical guidelines on how to do so. The second section consists of two chapters that extend these concepts to common challenges we face when traveling. These chapters illustrate how responsible travel practices can help us manage problems along the road. In the ninth chapter, Ellie Cleary tackles issues faced by women travelers. Finally, the last three chapters of the book focus on the broader question of making travel sustainable, socially responsible, and a tool for peacemaking and social betterment.

In short, the book makes the case for travel—but not just any travel. The goal of the book is to explore how we can create travel experiences that are sustainable and mutually beneficial. It provides strategies for how we can connect with others abroad and provides tips on using these experiences to create positive change (tips summarized in bullet points at the end of each chapter).

So why travel responsibly? In a world of conflict and polarization, more than ever, travel can be a tool for positive change—but only if that travel is done respectfully and reflectively. Travel thus has to start with a change of heart and a new frame of mind. Whether spending time with those who hold different political opinions or meeting members of different ethnic communities, travel must begin with a willingness to listen and learn.

We might think the other side has nothing to say worth hearing; we might think the divides are too wide to cross. But if Israelis and Palestinians can "travel" to the other side (in the context of one of the most infamously intractable conflicts in the world), anyone can. Reflecting on our own travel practices, and being willing to hear new perspectives, is thus the first step to responsible, transformative travel—and the first step to a more peaceful world.

CHAPTER 2

THE CASE FOR (RESPONSIBLE) TRAVEL

THERE ARE MANY good arguments against tourism, starting from its negative environmental impact, irresponsible practices, cultural insensitivity, and abuse of locals. Airline travel is estimated to contribute 2 percent of greenhouse emissions.[1] In the Mediterranean region, where fresh water is a major issue, tourists at times use double the amount of water as locals. The World Wildlife Fund reported in June 2018 that tourists visiting the Mediterranean during the summer produce a 40 percent increase in plastic entering the sea.[2]

These arguments make a good case against irresponsible travel and should encourage us to take a serious look at the practices of the travel industry. However, we also should be aware of the positive impact that travel can have. Many economies depend significantly on travel; the travel industry generates 1 in every 10 jobs around the world, for instance.[3] It also accounts for 10 percent of the world's global activity.[4] And as this book will explore, travel can have social benefits—if done correctly.

That said, the travel industry has a long road ahead to become sustainable. Stories from around the world testify to the problems. Venetians report that their city is so overcrowded with tourists, most local businesses (butchers, florists, bakeries, Murano glass manufacturers) have shuttered because they can't afford the rent. Locals don't even see the money—the tour buses take their loads of tourists to big souvenir outlets on the edge of town, which sell fake Murano glass made in China. Many cruise ship companies are causing significant problems in their travel destinations. Belize has become overrun with cruise ship passengers, who spend an average of $44 per day on land and stay only one day (as opposed to land passengers, who spend $96 per day and stay seven days), and locals report that the ships are causing damage to wildlife and coral reefs. In Cozumel, local tour operators pay up to 50 percent of their profit for advertising on certain cruise ships.[5]

Although more governments and travel operators have started tackling major issues like tourist overcrowding, the environmental impact of tourism, and income inequalities, problems still abound. So is there a solution in sight?

Why Do We Travel?

Hasso Spode, who heads the historical archive on tourism at the Free University of Berlin, differentiates between the old and new ways of traveling. Until recently, travel, according to Spode, always incorporated a mission. "The pilgrims, for example, wanted to find salvation; the conquistadors wanted to conquer." Tourism today, however, often doesn't include a mission and is purely for leisure.[6]

But not all who journey abroad go on tours without a purpose. We should distinguish between tourists—who travel "just for fun"—and travelers, who seek an educational and cultural experience on their trips.

Educational travel is an ancient kind of journey that remains alive today. I grew up hearing the old Islamic saying "Seek education even if in China"—and China is really far from the Middle East.

Travel today doesn't have to be without purpose. In reality, the only way for travel to be responsible and justifiable is when it has a purpose. This doesn't mean that travelers can't have fun, enjoy the beach, and do some sightseeing. It means that this shouldn't be the only purpose for our travels.

I never see myself as just a tourist. I am a traveler who uses my trips as an opportunity to learn and connect to the world. I decided to become involved in the travel industry because I saw its potential for major social change. If we can change the way people travel, we can change the world.

Travel is the world's biggest exchange program, and it has the potential to similarly be its biggest educational program. During my first trip to Lebanon in 2015, I hired a driver to take me to Byblos, one of the oldest seaports in the world. Josef, the driver, was a Lebanese man with short white hair and a youthful glow that beamed from behind the wrinkles on his face.

He was witty and had a talent for sharing stories. He liked to talk, and I had many questions about his well-kept 1960 red Mercedes. He told me that he had owned the car since it was made. He boasted that he had never had to change the engine. He said that he took care of the car as if she were part of his family.

He then began describing his journeys to and from Germany, back when he bought the car in 1960. He said that, back then, you could travel from Lebanon to Germany, buy a car, and drive it back to Lebanon. He drove through Europe, Turkey, and Syria. He could even drive his car to Jerusalem for the weekend without a problem. This would be impossible today because borders have changed, and many countries wouldn't allow Josef to travel through them. Josef painted a vastly different portrait of the Middle East than what I was used to. He inspired me to dream that perhaps one day this could happen again, and I could travel to Germany and drive back to Jerusalem with a new BMW.

A person's life can be shaped by travel experiences. So why not make travel educational and inspirational? Travel educates us and challenges us, but it also dares us to dream, to imagine a better future. There is so much hope, kindness, and goodness in the world, which can be discovered through travel. For me, that's why I started a travel company and became an advocate for reforming the travel industry. I've tried to push it toward adopting a sustainable framework, which takes into account the travelers, the locals, and the environment.

Should Everyone Travel?

"Do we really want everyone in the US to travel abroad? Can we afford that environmentally?" my friend Peter, who lives in DC, asked me. "And what about insensitive and ignorant people? They don't seem to care, and they cause trouble. They also tarnish the image of America abroad."

With overcrowding at many European tourist sites, this is a common criticism I hear. But I believe tourism promotion should not be focused on increasing the number of travelers; there are already many people traveling across the world. Instead, what we should be focusing on is changing *how* people travel.

Overtourism is a major problem in some destinations, but undertourism is also a problem—sometimes within a half-hour driving distance. When I visited Barcelona, Spain, for the first time in 2016 for a travel conference, I walked around the city and noticed that I didn't hear anyone speaking Catalan, the local language. Instead, all the conversations I heard were in English or other languages. The city was filled with tourists who rarely got to meet locals, never mind speak to them. One Barcelona resident I met at the conference told me that he felt like a guest in his own city. It made sense, considering that Barcelona, a city of 1.6 million residents, receives 32 million tourists every year.

The Catalan government now has to battle these issues. Locals can no longer afford living in certain areas of the city, where housing prices have increased by more than 50 percent in the last five years.

The government was recently forced to pass a law that caps rent increases and ties rent to inflation, which currently stands at 1.5 percent. In 2014, the government attempted to tackle the issue of affordable housing in the city. It stopped issuing new licenses for vacation apartments, leaving approximately 9,600 apartments with a license to rent to tourists. A recent agreement with Airbnb allowed the company's rental data to be shared with the government to prevent unlicensed apartments from being listed on the site.

A recent social media campaign asked travelers to verify that their vacation rentals were legal and report those that were not. This issue of overtourism should make us as travelers reexamine our travel destinations and our relationships with local communities. In 2002, 280 delegates from 20 countries met in Cape Town, South Africa, to discuss responsible tourism practices. At the end of the conference, they issued a declaration that addressed world travel issues, including the problems in Catalonia. As the document declared, "What is good for citizens is good for the tourist. Places that are good to live in are also good to visit. The tourist that Catalonia wants to attract is the one who will respect the environment, the society, and the local culture, [and who is] eager to discover and share experiences."

In 2019, I visited Igualada, a small town about one hour away from Barcelona, for the purpose of meeting with the local community to discuss strategies that would attract tourists to spend more time on the outskirts of Barcelona. These villages outside of the city are interested in developing tourism experiences and see it as a valuable opportunity for economic development.

Locals in Barcelona have gotten fed up with tourism and want tourists out of their city, but just a 40-minute drive away there are beautiful villages where locals are eager to receive these tourists. While in Igualada, I met with the mayor and other leaders from the towns nearby, along with local business owners, community leaders, and young entrepreneurs—all of whom are working together on ideas to attract tourists to their towns.

The solution for overtourism doesn't have to be no tourism. Tourism is still a major part of Catalonia's economy. Many smaller towns in the region would love to welcome travelers. Traveling to Barcelona is still possible if we take into account the challenges and complaints of the residents, but a better solution would be to spend part of our vacation in the smaller villages outside Barcelona.

Similarly, I recently visited Dubrovnik, Croatia, where my friend the photojournalist Ziyah Gafic took me to meet with Wade Goddard, another photojournalist, who founded War Photo Limited—a photo gallery that exhibits war-related photography from the Balkans and other regions. Croatia saw 57,587,000 tourists in 2016 in an area with a population of 4,170,600. There are 14 tourists for every local, making Croatia the country with the largest number of tourists to locals.

Overtourism has gotten so bad that UNESCO threatened to remove Dubrovnik's World Heritage Site status unless Croatia implemented changes that would reduce the number of tourists in the city.[7] Wade, who is originally from New Zealand but has lived in the Balkans since the early '90s, explained that locals are tired of the crowded streets.

Growing cruise ship tourism has also caused the local tourism sector to suffer. Dubrovnik once attracted "seasoned" tourists, Wade said—tourists who spent several days or weeks in the medieval city and appreciated its breathtaking architecture and history. But now flocks of tourists are coming to the city just for one day. They don't eat in local restaurants; they hardly see anything outside the old city. They just line up to take a photo imitating the famous image of King's Landing at the city's seaport.

Although the cruise lines and the *Game of Thrones* craze have attracted more tourists to the city, they have not benefited the locals. The change is palpable: Dubrovnik's old city has only 1,500 people living there, as opposed to 5,000 in the early '90s.

"I swear, I think if I hear one more tourist call the old city 'King's Landing,' I'm just going to pack up my things and leave," Wade said, frustrated. You can't blame him. The ships that dock in Dubrovnik are the megaships, which dwarf the old limestone buildings and the Franjo Tuđman Bridge. Cruise ship tourism— which usually involves up to 6,000 passengers *per ship* debarking for just a few hours to explore the tiny old town—combined with *Game of Thrones* tourism has thus turned the local economy upside down. Tourists are no longer staying for a week to take in the history and culture of the city and enjoy the countryside wineries. Instead, local business owners are lucky if tourists decide to stay for more than one night.

Cruise ships don't only bring a load of tourists—they also are major polluters. In Dubrovnik, the cruise ships release significantly more pollution into the air than all the cars in the city. In Barcelona, cruise ships release five times more sulphur oxide than all of Barcelona's cars put together. In June 2019,

Barcelona was named the most polluted port in Europe, in part due to the cruise ships. These environmental challenges should be addressed and regulated. As travelers, we need to think more about our carbon footprint and how much pollution we generate by our choice of travel. Cruise ships have become a major tourism provider, but they must address their carbon footprint, their environmental and economic impact, and the level of their engagement with local communities.

A Shift in Strategy

It's important for governments to change their tourism advertising strategies by promoting meaningful travel. Similarly, travel agencies must hold themselves responsible and promote travel that doesn't just add carbon footprints without any positive outcomes. There are positive steps in this direction. In 2019, the Netherlands' tourism board announced that it would stop promoting the country for new tourists because it anticipated that 29 million tourists would arrive annually to the country by 2030, compared with 19 million now. The tourism board is focusing on managing tourism instead of promoting it, while encouraging people to go to less visited sites in the Netherlands—instead of creating a bottleneck in Amsterdam.[8]

More countries and cities around the world will need to follow in the Netherlands' footsteps. The only way to keep tourism sustainable is to manage it and ensure that we are not hurting the sites and destinations we visit.

We, the travelers, also have a responsibility in tackling overtourism. The world is bigger than we can imagine. Yet, we too often feel pressured to visit the same sites that our neighbors, friends, family, and coworkers have visited. In some cases, we don't even share the same interests with these people, but we find ourselves visiting the same destinations, eating at the same restaurants, swimming at the same beaches, and doing the same sightseeing.

We are also swayed by advertisements, celebrities, Instagram photos, and "influencers" on social media. Every now and then we read articles with titles like "Ten Destinations You Must Visit Before You Die" and "Most Beautiful Sites in Europe." These articles sell us one of the biggest lies in the travel industry. Some sites are rarely visited until they are featured in a movie, appear on the cover of a famous magazine, or are added to the World Heritage Sites list. Then, suddenly, they become major attractions. But there are breathtaking sites all over the world that are not featured in movies or magazines.

In 2019, I attended an education conference in Bali and decided to stay for a few days to explore the island. I have always seen the famous "Gate of Heaven" Instagram photos: pictures of tourists posing in a Balinese gate. Here, the local temple discovered that if they used a mirror to create an illusion of a lake reflection, travelers would come. And come they did: today, travelers spend four to five hours round trip driving to and from the temple. At the temple, they wait in line for at least two hours (and often longer) to take one photo—which may or may not look good, depending on weather conditions. I couldn't believe that people would waste a full day of their trip standing in line for this. I asked our driver what he thought about it, and he said, "I don't understand why tourists go there. There are a few other temples that provide a similar photo opportunity at a gate with a mirror. But everyone sees this photo on Instagram, wakes up at 5 a.m., and drives out to the same place to stand in line. If they ask, we can give them other options." I tested one of these alternative temples, and sure enough, we drove right up and were able to re-create almost the same photo in five minutes—leaving plenty of time for meeting locals and exploring the religious traditions of the area.

When we fall for the trap of visiting famous sites just because they are famous, we make tourism unsustainable, and eventually we contribute to the destruction of these sites that we claim to like and care about. I'm often asked by friends, "Where is the best place to travel to?" or "What is your favorite destination?" or "Where should I go?" My answer is always that it depends on what you like, what you care about, and what's important to you.

I also encourage people to visit the less traveled destinations. The size of the crowd visiting a destination shouldn't be the reason you travel there. In fact, the size of the crowd at a destination is often a reason to avoid it, because you won't go away happy, and you'll end up being a burden to the locals and part of the problem. It is important to realize that more often than not, there is zero correlation between the size of the crowds visiting a destination and the beauty, culture, and experience the destination has to offer.

Be Aware: Travel Is a Privilege

Many people around the world can't travel. Some can't travel for financial reasons, and others can't travel because their passport or government doesn't allow them to. My nephew Eyad is a Jerusalem resident who wanted to take his first international trip last month. Like me, Eyad was born without any citizenship. He has only a handful of destinations he can visit without applying for a visa, and should he apply, he would likely be rejected because of his citizenship status (which for Jerusalem Palestinians is "undefined").

As a Palestinian resident of Jerusalem, I didn't have a regular passport growing up. That said, I engaged with the world without ever leaving Jerusalem. As a teenager, I tried to speak with tourists to practice English and to learn about the world beyond my city. I had no citizenship. I used to joke that I was a citizen of the world, but in reality, not many countries would give me a visa. Learning to travel in my hometown thus became important to me because it allowed me still to connect with the world around me. The world came to me when I couldn't go see it.

I am a Jerusalem resident—often referred to as a Jerusalemite—but not an Israeli citizen. Applying for Israeli citizenship is possible for Jerusalemites, but very difficult. According to the news outlet *The Times of Israel*, as of September 2016, Palestinian Jerusalemites had submitted 1,102 applications for Israeli citizenship that year, and only nine applications were approved. Two were rejected—the rest waiting years in limbo for their applications to be processed (a way of rejecting valid applications without raising questions and the rejections being logged in official statistics).[9]

Not having Israeli citizenship meant that I also couldn't get an Israeli passport. Instead, I was given an Israeli travel document and a Jordanian travel document (because Jerusalem was under Jordanian authority until 1967). Traveling as a stateless, young Middle Eastern man was a nightmare. You have to plan your trip months in advance and apply for visas that necessitate showing dozens of documents: bank statements, proof of employment, background checks, prepurchased round-trip airline tickets, prepurchased hotel reservations, invitation letters and sponsorship letters, letters of character, health records, and documents proving an official purpose for your visit—paying hefty nonrefundable fees for a trip that might ultimately be rejected.

This headache was then followed by weeks or sometimes months of waiting for a response. More often than not, I was denied; all of that money and work collecting documents were often for nothing. For someone who travels often for work, I was handcuffed by this process; my work suffered because of my inability to travel. Applying for a visa became a very stressful procedure; each time I went through it, I knew that I was likely to be rejected.

When I was invited to speak in Budapest, Hungary, for instance, my visa was rejected because the consulate thought there was a chance I would lodge an asylum request upon my arrival in the country. Even when my visa application was accepted to some countries, it was only after numerous calls to those who could vouch for me.

This was my normal travel experience: a continuous hassle for a visa.

This is the reality of most people in the world, but those with first-world passports tend not to comprehend this struggle. I have experienced both sides of this reality. I received my US citizenship and US passport in 2015, and since then, my travel life has completely transformed. I flew to Amman a few weeks after getting the passport and had a long layover in Frankfurt, Germany. For the first time in my life, I was able to leave a transit airport and meet up with friends. Suddenly, I was not a problem anymore.

If that trip had been just five weeks earlier, I wouldn't have been able to leave the airport. Now, however, I can travel almost anywhere in the world, and if a visa is required, it's often just a formality or I can get it on arrival.

Travelers Can Positively Impact Their Destinations

When Peter, the friend in Washington, DC, asked me if I wanted people who were culturally insensitive to travel, I felt like I was trapped in a paradox. On one hand, I don't want people who are disrespectful to travel. During my last trip to Cancun for another travel conference, I got into a discussion with four older Americans who were making racist comments about Mexicans—in Mexico. I felt embarrassed and upset.

However, I also know that travel is the best chance for these individuals to examine their biases and racist attitudes—if they'll just step outside their resort. When we travel, we are confronted with what we really believe. We are able to examine our biases. I don't think it is my right to decide who deserves to travel and who doesn't, but I believe in providing the tools to travelers that can help them have a meaningful trip where they can expand their knowledge, reexamine their biases, and, most important, care about people and the destinations they visit.

Travel expands our horizons and helps us learn new things. Belize is a destination that is world famous for snorkeling and diving. When I arrived in the country, I was excited to swim, snorkel, and explore the caves in the interior. I also felt, however, that if I cared about snorkeling and the country's environment, then I should also take the time to learn about the challenges facing these pristine seas.

What can be done to help preserve destinations like Belize? I am very grateful for my friend Enric Sala, a National Geographic Explorer who taught me about the role of tourism in saving our oceans. In his TED Talk, Enric spoke about the potential power of tourism in protecting the oceans without harming the fishermen:

> In 1999, a little place called Cabo Pulmo in Mexico was an underwater desert. The fishermen were so upset not having enough fish to catch that they did something that no one expected. Instead of spending more time at sea, trying to catch the few fish left, they stopped fishing completely. They created a national park in the sea. A no-take marine reserve. When we returned, 10 years later, this is what we saw. What had been an underwater barren

was now a kaleidoscope of life and color. We saw it back to pristine in only 10 years, including the return of the large predators, like the groupers, the sharks, the jacks, and those visionary fishermen are making much more money now, from tourism. Now, when we can align economic needs with conservation, miracles can happen.[10]

According to Enric, the ocean's beauty is what brings people to the beaches of Belize. Tourism is a foundational economic industry for Belize, making up 38 percent of the country's GDP. If Belize loses its fish, it loses its tourism. It is no wonder that Belize is a leader in marine protection. According to the *Guardian*, Belize has recently increased its "'no-take zones' in its marine protected areas from 4.5% to 11.6%."[11]

Because I took the time to learn and talk to people about how Belize has developed since independence in 1981, when I returned home, I didn't talk only about my snorkeling experience. I also became an ambassador for the environmental protection of our oceans. I learned to care!

Travel Can Solve the Biggest Threat

During an interview with the British newspaper the *Independent*, Stephen Hawking outlined the biggest threat to humanity, and it was not what most would have expected. It wasn't an asteroid hitting the Earth that worried Hawking. It wasn't even the environmental crisis that we're facing. Instead, it was human aggression. "The human failing I would most like to correct is aggression," he said. "It may have had survival advantage in caveman days, to get more food, territory, or a partner with whom to reproduce, but now it threatens to destroy us all." According to the *Independent*, Hawking especially wanted humans to focus on empathy to safeguard our future.[12]

Hawking understood that major threats to humanity can be dealt with if we learn to work together; none of our issues will be solved if we continue fighting and killing each other. This is what makes travel important. It's the largest exchange program in the world. It provides a huge opportunity to learn about each other and understand one another, which leads to our empathizing with each other. Travel is thus an effective avenue for promoting peace and understanding. If we can overcome aggression against each other, we can likely overcome the other threats facing humanity, guaranteeing a better future for the next generations.

Hawking's message is particularly important amid growing nationalism around the world, in which individuals are told to always put their own interests first. We are told that we are in the midst of a global competition, in which there will be winners and losers—and our country must win.

But we all live on this earth together, and what happens in China will affect people living thousands of miles away in Uruguay. Similarly, what happens in the United States impacts the lives of billions of people around the world. We don't live on islands isolated from the rest of the world's political problems, climate policies, economic situations, and threats. The issues facing human society do not recognize the artificial boundaries and borders we've created. We are all connected.

Is There a Case for Travel?

In the end, travel has the potential to destroy communities. But it also can help us care more about the world and understand that we are not isolated from those who live in a different city or country. It can make us care about people who look different from us.

In conflict resolution, the contact hypothesis theory suggests that "an interaction between individuals belonging to different groups will reduce ethnic prejudice and intergroup tension," as Stephen Ryan writes in *Ethnic Conflict and International Relations*.[13] But Ryan qualifies this: to reduce prejudice, contact between different groups must be based on equality and respect. So, if the 1.4 billion people who cross international borders every year traveled responsibly and fostered real, intimate connections with the people in the destinations they visited, imagine what would happen to our world! We must understand the privilege of travel, and therefore the responsibility we have in bringing down barriers and building bridges between our peoples. If we accept Hawking's claim that human aggression is a major threat to human existence, then I don't know a better medium than travel to promote understanding and coexistence. We, the travelers, have more power to better this world than we can even comprehend.

This, I believe, makes traveling worth it—as long as we're mindful of what impact we're having on the world. We have to ask ourselves three honest questions:

- How is my travel impacting me?
- How is my travel impacting the communities I visit?
- How is my travel impacting the environment?

If one is just traveling for the sake of getting drunk on a cruise and taking selfies, then I don't believe the pollution from that travel is worth it. But if one is traveling with the purpose of breaking boundaries, making connections, exchanging knowledge and culture, and learning from other societies and places, then there's a good argument that this travel is worthwhile.

Finally, since not everyone is able to travel, we should consider how we are using our travel experiences to connect with other people. Travelers can use their journeys to reach out to others who can't travel, both at home and abroad. Share your stories—and become part of the largest cultural exchange program in the world, because your next vacation can have more power than official diplomacy in connecting the world and bridging differences.

CHAPTER 3

WHAT DOES RESPONSIBLE TRAVEL LOOK LIKE?

"RESPONSIBLE TOURISM IS about using tourism to make better places for people to live in and better places for people to visit, in that order." This is how Dr. Harold Goodwin, cochair of the International Conferences on Responsible Tourism in Destinations, describes responsible tourism in an essay on his website.[1]

Harold Goodwin explains that everyone involved in the travel industry—including the travelers—must take responsibility for making the industry more sustainable. I agree with him. Taking personal responsibility for your impact on the places you visit is an important aspect of sustainable travel. Sustainable travel happens when all stakeholders, including governments, travel agencies, and travelers, come together to financially, environmentally, and socially make a positive impact on travel destinations. He argues that we can move toward responsibility by minimizing our negative economic, environmental, and social impacts.

Evaluating Tours That Claim
to Be Socially Responsible

During my first trip to Vietnam in 2016, I was looking for experiences that went beyond the usual sightseeing tours. I hired a guide who offered to bring us to a Vietnamese family's home for tea. I agreed and found myself in the living room of an elderly Vietnamese couple. I first met Madame Xon, who was 90 years old but still healthy and active. She was stunningly beautiful, with a big smile. Her lips were dark red because she had consumed a betel nut. Her welcoming spirit was palpable, and she was genuinely happy to have guests in her house.

As soon as I greeted her, she grabbed my hand and walked me through the house to the backyard, where her 92-year-old husband was watering crops. We stood outside and talked about their lives as farmers, with my guide serving as a translator. I was eager to know how long they had lived there and how they were able to take care of the land. We also talked about the rough times, during the American-Vietnamese war.

We had an amazing conversation. Even when the guide was unable to translate, I felt that words didn't matter; we connected on a human level. I never got to meet my grandparents because they died before I was born. But in that moment, I felt this was what it would have been like to have my grandparents alive.

This couple didn't shy away from showing affection for each other. They enjoyed sitting outside and watching over the land, their crops, and the people passing by. The husband joked that in the afternoon he got a couple of beers and sat down to enjoy the beauty of nature. "Beer is the secret to a long life," he said with a wide smile and a playful wink.

These two had been married for more than 70 years, and yet I don't think I have ever met a couple who looked at each other with so much warmth and passion. They laughed, held hands, and helped each other water the plants. They had a lot to teach about relationships, love, and companionship; they seemed to have figured out the secret to happiness.

At the end of our discussion, however, I found myself wondering whether the visit was being operated in a responsible way. I looked at the guide and asked him how much this couple was being paid for our visit. He said, "Don't worry, we pay them fine."

I decided to pry. "OK, but how much exactly do you pay them?" He finally admitted that he paid the couple just $1 to spend time and chat with tourists.

All too often, tour guides and other industry players take advantage of customers, vendors, and the communities they visit. In recent years, "fair trade" products and "socially responsible" initiatives have cropped up in almost every industry, and some of these are outstanding initiatives. But not every tour that claims to be socially responsible actually does what it says.

In the Vietnamese case above, the company claimed they were contributing to the community in a responsible way. And they might have believed that what they were paying was fair. They would argue that the economic desperation the community is experiencing makes even 50 cents sufficient payment. Tour operators will also say that it's important not to overpay, because that creates an unbalanced economy—especially in lower-income areas. There is some truth to this.

But just because a community is willing to accept scraps in exchange for participating in the travel industry does not make this a fair business practice. As travelers, we should always be asking ourselves how much of our money is going to support the local community. These experiences that connect you to local people are important, but it's just as important for these initiatives to benefit those local people directly. As a result, we need to ask questions about where our money is going. How much are the communities benefiting from our tourism? How much margin is the company making off the trip? How well are organizations or speakers being reimbursed for their work? Are vendors and guides being paid a fair wage, or are they being forced to work longer hours than is safe and reasonable? What are the average paycheck and employment rate? A quick web search or conversation with your tour operator can answer all of these questions.

But often we are too shy to ask these questions. We are quick to trust our tour operators because they claim to be "a responsible tour company" or because their website boasts about donating a certain percentage of their profit to charities. We build connections with the tour guide and feel that asking such questions might be disrespectful.

It's not. On the contrary, asking such questions is respectful and shows that you care. I am happy when our travelers ask me these questions. I want them to know that their trip is not a burden on locals but actually helping local organizations, individuals, and communities.

One of the most misleading trends among some travel companies is purporting to be responsible because of their charity donations. Does it really matter that you donate 5 percent or even 10 percent of your profit if you don't pay your vendors fairly? I've had this conversation with a few tour operators, and my argument is that it's better to stop giving that 5 percent to charity and to pay the guides, the speakers, the hosts, the drivers, the bellboy, and everyone working for you more fairly. And obviously, it's even better if you can do both!

Responsible travel means measuring how we treat the people we work with and how much we care about them. If you don't care about the people who work with you, then you probably don't care about an NGO that you're donating to at the end of the year.

Travel companies adapt such practices because it's much easier to use those donations as a stamp of approval and a marketing strategy to get more customers than it is to actually apply responsible practices in the operation of their business.

So when you take your next tour, don't be afraid to ask questions. Ask about payments to guides, drivers, and vendors, and to hosts you meet on the tour. This is the only way we will push more and more businesses to operate responsibly.

In the case of the Vietnamese couple, when I realized they weren't being paid to the standards I believed were fair, I asked the tour guide if there was a way I could give money in a culturally acceptable way—without inadvertently offending the couple. I didn't want them to feel this money was charity, because it wasn't: they deserved it. However, I needed to be culturally sensitive and appropriate.

I was lucky. It was the Vietnamese New Year (Tet), and it is customary during this time for individuals to visit one another and leave a red envelope of cash for family. So after finding a bright red flowery Tet envelope, I added some extra money, went back to their house, and gave it to the grandmother, wishing her a Happy New Year ("Chúc Mừng Năm Mới!") in an unintentionally terrible accent that made her laugh.

Support Equitable Initiatives
Run by Locals

In a confidential letter in 1949, a British official named Ronald Fay who was visiting Luxor wrote to the British Embassy in Cairo with a dire report: "The hotels are fuller than they have been for many years, as a great many local tours are being organized and BOAC [British Overseas Airways Corporation] boats make a night stop at Luxor. However, those tourists spend little money in the local shops, and it is only the hotels and a few dragomen [Egyptian guides] who are benefiting. This is giving rise to a certain amount of xenophobia."[2]

Even back in 1949, there was a struggle between responsible and irresponsible tourism. In his letter, Fay connected the bad practices of tourism with growing xenophobia and antagonism toward tourists. The Muslim Brotherhood at that time took advantage of this situation to recruit new members and sent threatening letters to hotels demanding that they stop showing foreign films. However, Fay seemed to intuitively grasp that the real issue had less to do with politics or religious affairs and more to do with the way tourism and foreign visitors were changing the lives of locals but benefiting only a few.

Harold Goodwin explains that responsible tourism "generates greater economic benefits for local people and enhances the well-being of host communities. [It] improves working conditions and access to the industry. [It] involves local people in decisions that affect their lives and life chances."[3]

The tourism industry at times misses the mark on this one. Its focus is often on maximizing profits, regardless of the cost for local communities. In order to transform the travel industry, we should be moving toward partnering with locals to create a mutually sustainable relationship.

In conflict resolution, we know that unequal economic development causes division and conflict in local communities. So, when we create conditions in which locals feel like they are being taken advantage of, we promote anger, conflict, resentment, and xenophobia. These feelings eventually find their way back to the tourists, because we cannot visit and enjoy a country when the locals resent our presence.

So how do we seek out and support travel experiences that don't breed local resentment?

On my last trip to Colombia, I visited Cartagena for the first time and met with Andrea, a friend of a friend who is working to promote responsible tourism in the region. Andrea introduced me to the coastal city and to Afro-Colombians who live there. Throughout my time in Cartagena, I learned about Afro-Colombian history and culture, discovering how the community was made up of descendants of those kidnapped from Africa and brought to Colombia as slaves.

Approximately 10 percent of Colombia's current population is Afro-Colombian. In Cartagena they are more than a third of the population. When slavery was abolished in 1851, Afro-Colombians gained freedom but inherited poverty—shaped by lack of development and resources in their communities. Today, Colombia is among the worst countries when it comes to unequal land distribution; as a result, the Afro-Colombian community has suffered significantly.

When the constitution was rewritten in 1991, an article was added to expand the indigenous collective titles of land law to include the Afro-Colombian communities. However, it's a 14-step process, which includes filing a request that can take up to 20 years to get approved. Approximately 80 Afro-Colombian communities have filed for a collective title for their land, and only 7 communities have received it so far—but there are more than 800 Afro-Colombian and indigenous communities across Colombia (many of whom are not even aware of the existence of this law).

Andrea had been involved in Fem, a local Colombian non-profit organization that works to help Afro-Colombian communities apply for the collective land titles while creating employment opportunities for community members (since the average wage for an Afro-Colombian is three times lower than that of other Colombians). Poverty and lack of options is often cited as the reason for the high recruitment rate among Afro-Colombians into guerrilla and paramilitary groups. In fact, a 2005 study found that due to lack of employment among Afro-Colombians, up to 40 percent of paramilitary and guerrilla recruits were African descendants in coastal regions.[4]

Fem realized that they needed to think outside the box to tackle the unemployment rate in the region. Cartagena is a hot tourism destination, yet the Afro-Colombian community hasn't benefited from it. As a result, Fem established Cartagena Insider, a travel agency that helps Afro-Colombians provide tourism services to travelers.

Cartagena Insider trains former combatants from paramilitary groups to become part of a growing tourism industry. Some of them are trained to be tour guides, cooks, and dance instructors, among other trades. Tourism has thus become a way for these fighters to reintegrate into the community.

As an example of their work, Andrea introduced me to young artists who were offering dancing sessions to teach about Colombian music and generate income to help support the local school. Other community members were teaching travelers how to make traditional sombrero vueltiao hats, using a special material called *caña flecha*. Being strongly connected to nature, the community also offers trekking experiences, mangrove expeditions, and bird-watching tours in the protected area in partnership with local fishermen.

These fishermen also need tourism badly, because they are being pushed out by new developments. Travelers provide visibility to their community and help the fishermen pressure the government by showcasing the contribution these fishermen make. Travelers are able to support these fishermen financially and highlight the social justice issues they're facing. The fishermen believe that the government will back off from some of the development projects if it sees a major increase of tourism in the area. In this way, travelers can be social activists in the destinations they visit.

This is exactly the kind of responsible tourism that Harold Goodwin and the Cape Town Declaration have worked to promote. Andrea and her colleague Ana Maria are making sure their tourism project isn't negatively impacting the culture or environment of the local area. They are working with multiple communities to avoid flooding one community (Cartagena) with all the tourists. They don't use plastic or other polluters on their excursions, and they support local Afro-Colombian communities.

When I asked them how a traveler would find them, they said that marketing themselves was a major challenge. Travelers should not just look for well-known brand names when booking a tour, but instead seek certified, vetted local operators and organizations that are known to be applying responsible principles. In Colombia, for example, Acotur is an association for responsible tourism and guides travelers to organizations and companies across the country that practice responsible tourism.[5]

Before traveling to any destination, one concrete step you can take is to check if your destination has an association like Acotur. The Global Sustainable Tourism Council (GSTC) has criteria for both tour operators and destinations that help define responsible companies we can use when booking our vacations.

GSTC Criteria for tour operators are divided into four categories:

1. **Sustainable business management practices:** Complying with local laws, license requirements, and permit requirements; using low-impact transportation; having a system in place for accepting and responding to customer feedback; using honest marketing/advertising practices; using sustainable materials in offices and buildings (for example, not keeping lawns that require large amounts of water in drought-prone areas); informing customers about appropriate behavior for the destination; educating customers on the area's cultural heritages.

2. **Practices that maximize social and economic benefits / minimize harm to the local community:** Employing locals

(and maintaining equal opportunity employment practices); paying fair and livable wages; buying from or pursuing partnerships with local vendors; engaging in local community initiatives; maintaining anti-harassment and anti-exploitation policies regarding vulnerable groups (and keeping employee records to show that no child labor or exploitation is occurring).

3. **Practices that maximize benefits / minimize harm to cultural heritage:** Following laws about artifacts (their use, handling, and display); not impeding open access to sites; working with locals in determining the size and frequency of group visits (in order to not overwhelm the capacity of sites); protecting indigenous communities and putting practices in place to protect local children against inappropriate or exploitative contact; complying with heritage preservation requirements.

4. **Practices that maximize benefits / minimize harm to the environment:** Buying from vendors with environmental certifications (especially regarding wood, paper, and fish products); purchasing recyclable goods / minimizing use of disposable and single-use products; stewarding water usage; reducing greenhouse gas emissions; appropriately disposing of waste; not introducing invasive species; not feeding wildlife; complying with local, national, and international regulations on wildlife interactions and viewing.[6]

When choosing a tour operator, you can also look for companies that are Certified B Corporations. B Corps undergo rigorous certification processes and must disclose financial and business records to verify that they are socially responsible toward workers, customers, suppliers, the community, and the environment. B Corps also (1) must be able to show that they have a social (not just financial) bottom line, (2) must recertify every two years, and (3) are rated on their performance in each of the target areas.[7]

If a company is not a B Corp, you can ask it about its community engagement strategy and business practices. Does the company offer any education, training, or job-creation programs? What is its mission statement? Is the company transparent about its social responsibility claims? What are its policies concerning staff compensation and benefits? And what is the company doing to be environmentally conscious?

Shop Responsibly

Another way to ensure that you have a positive impact is to shop —but shop responsibly!

When I visited Bogotá, I joined a tour that focused on indigenous groups working to escape cycles of violence and crime. On one of the stops, we visited a chocolate shop selling products made from cacao that had been planted by a community located a few hours' drive outside of Bogotá.

This community had decided to stop growing coca (cocaine) and grow cacao, from which chocolate is made, in its place. One of the farmers told me that although they had been making a "crazy" amount of money as local suppliers to the illicit drug industry, "it destroyed our communities."

"It destroyed who we were as a culture," he continued. "We became different people. We had more violence, and people were being killed. We realized that this is not working. We decided that we are going to change things." The community joined together and decided to start farming a different, legal crop: cacao. The villages around them thought they were insane.

"They told us we were stupid," he said. Other villages warned them that they would be cutting their profits dramatically; it wasn't possible to move from coca harvesting to cacao and maintain even close to the amount of profit they had received from the drug trade.

The group used some of the money they had made growing cocaine to invest in this chocolate shop in Bogotá. They branded the shop with their story—emphasizing how they had been able to escape the drug trade by shifting to cacao cultivation. Part of a tourist's visit to the shop is engaging with the group's stories.

They sell their products at a premium price, higher than the cost of mass-produced products. But they are not just selling a product; they are also selling an inspirational story and a chance to make a lasting impact. By buying their product, travelers participate in the peaceful effect the community is having in the country. Don't search for the lowest price you can pay for a local product. Despite the premium price, the farmers will be the first ones to tell you they are making much less money today than what they had once made in the illicit drug industry. However, although they were forced to cut their profits, their business is sustainable and successful—and most important, they can live their lives free of violence and fear.

The community is fully in charge—a central component of a socially responsible business. This is what should be promoted and supported in tourism. However, for these projects to succeed and make a difference, not only for one village but on a larger scale, more travelers are needed to visit and support these kinds of initiatives.

To promote more of this kind of tourism, we need to demand it from tourism agencies; we need to make it clear that we want to visit and support these communities. We, as travelers, must create this demand and request activities that forge a real connection with local people. It's not enough to pay and have a few locals come and perform for you. We need to be part of something bigger and more impactful.

Go Green

A final strategy you can use to make your travel more responsible is to go green. This doesn't only mean using recycled materials or avoiding plastic—being environmentally friendly can involve a variety of strategies.

For example, more tour operators, hotels, and buses are setting up water refilling stations offering filtered water. Travelers don't have to buy dozens of plastic water bottles on their trips. Instead, they can travel with their own refillable bottles. The more demand there is for these water refilling stations, the more we will see pop up. You can also choose to stay at a green hotel. Smaller, locally owned hotels are often a good way to go green. There are certifications for environmentally conscious establishments such as LEED-certified hotels.[8] You should also consider public transport as your main way to get around instead of renting a car wherever you go. These small steps do make a significant difference in shrinking our carbon footprints.

Finally, you can find activities that support environmental initiatives. For instance, in Cairo, we often take groups to Garbage City. Despite the uninviting name (stemming from the fact that the neighborhood is traditionally the place where poor Coptic Christian garbage collectors brought the city's trash), the neighborhood and its story is nothing short of inspiring. Once a neighborhood overflowing with piles of refuse many stories high, it is slowly being transformed by a new industry: recycling.

Every morning, lines of trucks enter Garbage City, carrying the trash of Cairo. After the community separates the trash into different kinds, colors, and sizes, it is sent to recycling workshops dotting the neighborhood. There are workshops for plastic, paper, metal, computer and electronic components, and so on. According to the community, 80 to 85 percent of the garbage that enters the community gets recycled—a rate higher than in most first-world countries, and double or even triple the rate compared with most recycling companies. It was hard for me to comprehend that this small neighborhood in North Africa beat first-world countries in recycling. And yet, they do.

During our tours, we connect with NGOs (nongovernmental organizations) in the neighborhood that take us to visit the workshops and speak with locals in the recycling business, who explain to us why recycling in Cairo is so important. Cairo is one of the largest cities in the world, and it has for years struggled with a garbage problem. The Garbage City residents are a major part of Cairo's garbage collection strategy. Women use the recycled material to make new products such as textiles, and the children learn about the recycling process in school.

The city is built from a local economy of recycling garbage. Predictably, there are parts of the neighborhood (dedicated to organic waste) that smell horrible. But that didn't make the city any less interesting; for me, it was the opposite. It was more interesting to be somewhere different—to see an entirely different side of Egypt and be part of helping make this project sustainable, while listening and understanding the challenges they face.

Travelers who visit Garbage City leave informed and transformed. About six years ago, I took my sister to the neighborhood for a visit. My sister, who lives in Cairo, at times helps me with our tours there. Stereotypes are pervasive in Egypt; for instance, many Muslims believe that all Egyptian Christians are wealthy, while most American Christians assume that all Egyptian Christians are poor (since many American churches visit the church near Garbage City and make contributions to the Christian community there). In fact, like most communities, Egyptian Christians are diverse. My Muslim sister was surprised when I took her to Garbage City and she saw that its Christian residents were far from wealthy. It is true that the richest Egyptians are

Christian, but that doesn't mean all Christians are wealthy. For my sister to see a neighborhood that defied her stereotypes of Christians had a major impact on her.

Similarly, the Christian residents flashed prolonged stares at my hijab-wearing sister during her visit. She quickly became self-conscious, realizing that she was the only woman in the neighborhood wearing a headscarf. She walked into the church, and I could see that the churchgoers were looking at her confusedly, thinking, "Why is this Muslim here?" And she was thinking, "Why am I here?"

But luckily the discomfort lasted only for about five minutes, and since then my sister has become good friends with several of the Christian residents, quickly overcoming the superficial divide that had initially created tension between them.

Becoming Responsible Travelers

Each of us is responsible for caring about the destinations we're visiting—and we are still responsible once we leave. Here are some fun and educational ways to travel more responsibly:

- Ask more questions of your tour operator about where your money is going. Choose a tour operator that pays fair wages to locals, and ask, "What percentage of the money I pay for my tour is being spent locally?"

- Evaluate tours that claim to be responsible, by taking five minutes to look at how the GSTC evaluates social responsibility for travel companies.

- Explore travel industry B Corps and their ratings.

- Support sustainable initiatives run by locals.

- Shop responsibly, and patronize underprivileged groups trying to break into the merchant economy.

- Go green, by cutting back on water usage and single-use plastics, and supporting environmental initiatives at the destination you are visiting.

There are of course many other ways to travel responsibly. When you find a vendor, hotel, destination, speaker, or tour operator that is being responsible, support their work by recommending them to others (and giving them positive reviews online). By being responsible travelers, we can inspire others to make similar choices.

We must take responsibility for changing how the travel industry operates. We, the travelers, create the demand for these tours, and therefore we can and should complain or withdraw our business when tour agencies, hotels, or even governments behave irresponsibly. It may mean an extra 30 minutes of planning, but by taking steps to travel responsibly, we can ensure that our money is benefiting local communities, and better contribute to the well-being of cultures, economies, and environments.

CHAPTER 4

DIVERSIFYING
YOUR ITINERARY

A FEW YEARS AGO, I was invited to give a workshop at Michigan State University (in East Lansing, Michigan) on designing study abroad programs. I wanted to highlight the importance of searching and exploring every destination in a holistic way. No place is homogeneous, and no country has a single story. While the cities and countries we visit are diverse, too often we end up hearing a single narrative—missing the complexity and multiplicity of stories that exist at the destination.

I started the workshop by dividing the attendees into three groups and asking them to create a hypothetical itinerary for exchange students touring East Lansing. What would each group want them to see? Whom should they meet, and what should they do?

East Lansing is a small city, with no more than 50,000 residents, and is a typical college town in the United States. For such a small town, would the workshop attendees send their students to the same well-known town landmarks?

Not only did the groups produce three different itineraries, but they each presented radically different schedules and activities. One group wanted their students to visit the main landmarks around the city, like the planetarium and the art museum. Another took the tour more toward culture and food, including places like the Ellison Brewery and the dairy store, a famous ice cream parlor (the group said it was a "must try"—I went straight there after the workshop to investigate, and they were absolutely right!). The third group focused on the university and issues facing the school, encouraging their imaginary student group to learn about challenges, such as the scandal surrounding Larry Nassar, a serial child molester who had worked for the university and was a former USA Gymnastics national team doctor. After the workshop, one of the participants modeled this for me and took me to a student protest objecting to the university leadership's response to the scandal.

Imagine, if the small town of East Lansing has so many different narratives, what stories do cities and countries have to tell? And if three small groups in East Lansing had different approaches and ideas about what travelers should see in their town, what might residents of foreign countries want us to see and learn about their cities?

When we travel abroad, many travelers will all adapt the same exact itinerary, leading all of them to the same places. Try an online search for tours to Italy, Israel, Egypt, Peru, or Vietnam, and you will find that most tours follow the same path, hitting the same landmarks, doing the same activities. Often the main difference is the price and the level of hotels. Shouldn't we wonder, does a country or city have only a few overcrowded, well-trodden sites to offer?

As a travel planner, I know that one of the reasons most itineraries follow the same path is laziness. It's convenient to do the same thing, visit the same sites, and eat the same food. It's more labor-intensive to look outside the box and explore. However, when you step out of the norm and take the road less traveled, places become infinitely more interesting, and the experience more meaningful and enriching.

Seek the Unheard Voices

The first step to breaking free from the usual itineraries is to actively look for the unheard stories, the voices that are not dominant in or are even missing from travel books. This requires a little research about the destination in order to learn about the different communities that live there. We should ask ourselves about minority groups and the disadvantaged—anyone who usually doesn't have a voice in the main narrative of a country.

Let's take Paris as an example. While the Eiffel Tower, Louvre, and Champs-Élysées are important national symbols and fun to visit, they are not the heart of France. Paris has much more to offer than just sites. The city is a major metropolitan center with incredible diversity. People from all over the world call Paris home, and there are huge, vibrant communities from former French colonies. My best time in Paris was taking a short ride to the African and Arab neighborhoods, where I found myself exploring a mix of Arab, African, and French cultures. I learned about the history of colonization and how these communities came to France. We talked about the people's journeys and their identities. Paris, like every destination, has more than one narrative—and if we are intentional in our travels, we can access these stories.

London is another great example. In London, it is wonderful to see Big Ben, explore the British Museum, and learn the history of Buckingham Palace and the royal family. However, London has other stories to tell. My friend Harold Goodwin, an expert on responsible tourism, recommends a company called Unseen

Tours, which hires homeless and formerly homeless people as tour guides. They describe their tours as tours *with* the homeless, not tours *of* the homeless. Participants learn about where London is excelling and where it is facing major social challenges. The guides explore London's history and culture and discuss tough issues in an unusual way, whereby no topic is off-limits.

These kinds of tours are a growing trend in Europe. In Athens, travelers can book with Shedia Invisible Tours, which also hires homeless and formerly homeless people to take you into the backstreets of the Greek capital and introduces you to local organizations working on social issues. Similarly, with Hidden City Tours in Barcelona, homeless and formerly homeless tour guides will take you on a food and market tour and to Montjuic to learn about culture and history. Similar concepts exist in Berlin, Prague, Vienna, and Amsterdam, among other cities.

As a traveler, if I want to advance peace wherever I travel, I must take the time to learn about social justice issues. I have to engage and support those who are on the frontier of tackling social problems at these destinations. This was much harder 20 years ago, but today, tourism has opened a door for us to explore cities in ways that we couldn't even imagine before. By taking one of these tours, we also financially support these individuals and communities, using tourism to transform their lives.

Take, for example, Maria, a tour guide with Shedia Invisible Tours, who explains how becoming a guide changed her life. "Having contact with the people is the greatest gift. I have become much more social. I was always a shy person. Today, I have gained a little more courage. It helps me to hear so good reviews. It encourages me to go ahead and try harder. I'm optimistic."[1]

It is important to point out that this is not poverty tourism. In poverty tourism, people travel to see poor areas and photograph poor people without any real engagement or respect for the community. It is voyeuristic and treats people as objects to be viewed for the traveler's edification. What I'm describing is seeking out tours conceived and operated by the community. Listening to people, hearing their stories, and showing them that we care about them is one of the greatest acts of peacemaking. Maria's testimony is a great example of that.

When we look at the conflicts in the world, too often we feel hopeless and helpless. We think about the magnitude of the problems facing our world. But by focusing on what we *can* do instead of focusing on what we *can't* do, we can help the destinations we visit. We can support social initiatives—and we can support people like Maria, as we grow in our understanding of how to make positive change.

Learn to Ask Questions

When my best friend and business partner, Scott Cooper, decided to step out of a preplanned itinerary, his life completely changed. I wanted to include Scott's story, in his own words, as a parallel to my own. Scott is an American Jew and the oldest of three. Even though his family was Jewish, they were not very religious and knew almost nothing about Israel. "The only thing we really knew about Israel is what we saw in the news—bombs, tanks, and war."

When Scott's youngest brother decided to go to Israel and live there for a year, the whole family was extremely worried. After months of his parents' pleading, Scott decided to use his two-week vacation to visit his brother in Israel, to see what he was doing there.

Scott was able to get a free trip through Birthright, which offers Jews 26 years old and younger a free trip to Israel. However like most tours, Birthright is limited in what it will show you about Israel: its aim is to make young Jews identify with the national narrative. But when the Birthright tour ended, Scott found himself with more questions than answers. He decided to meet with more local Israelis, including an Air Force captain, a security guard, and a few farmers. He was able to hear the stories of people he hadn't been exposed to on the tour.

By this time, Scott had already explored Israel more than most travelers would. But he still had questions. "At some point, I asked my Israeli friends about the conflict and the Palestinians. Most of them were scared, nervous, and had tragic personal stories," Scott recalled. But he was still not satisfied. So, he decided to go to Bethlehem, a Palestinian city. When he told his former tour guide that he was going there to meet with Palestinian peace activists, she froze and then started crying. She told him that he could get hurt, and he should not go.

Scott said, "I listened to what she had to say but decided to go anyway." He told me, "Once I boarded the Palestinian bus in Jerusalem toward Bethlehem, I was a bit scared. That fear dissipated pretty quickly, though. I remember that the first stop the bus made, some women got onto the bus and some teenage boys promptly jumped up and made room for them to sit. 'How courteous!' I thought. 'How often do we see this type of thing in the States?' . . . Once I got to Bethlehem, I met with Palestinians for the first time. We hit it off quickly."

Because of his experience with these new friendships, Scott decided to get involved with a group of local Palestinians and Israelis who were working together on peace-building efforts. What he found led him on the path he's still on with me today: working tirelessly for peace and justice.

Scott recounted,

That summer I met so many amazing people: young, old, religious, secular, Arab, Jewish, Christian, Druze, Israeli, and Palestinian, all working to end the conflict and make a better life there. One such meeting really sticks in my mind. I heard about this group of people who would get together to camp; have workshops; hear musical performances; and invite religious leaders, peace organizations, etc. It was called the Sulha, which I later found out was an Arabic word for "conflict resolution" or "mediation."

One of the workshops was for allowing teenagers —Palestinian and Israeli—to share in a safe space the traumatic experiences they'd had due to the conflict. I vividly remember attending one of these workshops; it was all in Hebrew and Arabic, so I couldn't understand.

But what I saw has stuck with me to this day. A young man shared a story and then abruptly stopped, started crying, and ran out of the tent. Right afterward, a young woman walked out to where he was, and you could hear her consoling him. I asked what had happened. As it turned out, the young man was from Gaza and had lost a family member recently due to the violence. The girl who ran after him was a 17-year-old Israeli girl about to join the army. I remember thinking that this entire conflict was on the back of these kids. . . . It inspired me to continue on this path of doing anything I could to support Israeli-Palestinian peace efforts."

Scott's unique experience of making friends with both Palestinians and Israelis, and seeing firsthand how those at the very center of the conflict could find a way to try to end it, motivated him to quit his job at a bank in Arizona. He moved to Northern Virginia to study conflict resolution at George Mason University. Of the decision, Scott says, "I felt that I had a moral obligation to support the locally led (and relatively unknown) efforts to create peace, justice, and reconciliation in the region."

I met Scott at the Center for World Religions, Diplomacy, and Conflict Resolution at George Mason, and our shared work in peace and conflict resolution inspired us to try building travel experiences. We hoped these experiences would give others the opportunity to travel the way Scott and I both had: going outside our comfort zones and listening to those who didn't always get to tell their story.

Scott understood the importance of not accepting talking points and of asking deeper questions. He also understood that he needed to travel to where he could find the answers to his questions.

What Scott was doing is called *track three diplomacy* in conflict resolution. According to Diana Chigas, a professor of the practice of international negotiation and conflict resolution at the Fletcher School of Law and Diplomacy, track three diplomacy is citizen diplomacy, which means "that peace can and must be built from the bottom up as well as from the top down. For any negotiation or settlement to be achieved, a 'peace constituency' must exist."[2]

In other words, travelers should see themselves as ambassadors while traveling and understand that their interactions with locals are part of building an international peace movement. As Chigas explains, citizen diplomacy strengthens moderate voices in the face of polarization. Even in times of conflict, spending time together, eating together, having drinks at the bar together, can change perceptions and break down stereotypes. As a result, citizen diplomacy is something all travelers can participate in, by asking questions, meeting "the other," and exchanging ideas.

Scott's life was changed by asking questions. And when I travel or build travel experiences, I follow the same principle. I start by asking tons of questions.

One excellent way to do this is to start conversations with your taxi drivers. Seek out people from different socioeconomic, ethnic, religious, and educational backgrounds. You can also talk to the people who work in your hotel, and to waiters and waitresses when you eat out. If you are inclined, you can further strike up conversations with fellow patrons. While visiting religious sites of different faiths or traditions, see if an attendant might be willing to talk with you.

I try to make these questions open-ended, because I want to make people feel comfortable sharing their stories. Probably the most common question I ask is "Can you tell me more about this?"

I ask about life stories, things like "Tell me more about your life, your childhood, your family. How did you end up where you are now (professionally or personally)?" I like to ask about stories that have impacted them, and why the story impacted them. I also ask about their vision of the future, their hopes and dreams, things that trouble them, and the issues and problems they face. Finally, I give them the opportunity to ask me questions.

This is a strategy used in peace building; we learn to ask less about people's political positions and more about their experiences. Stories tell us who people are, what they value, and how they got where they are now. It is much easier to connect to people (even if you disagree with them) when we are exchanging stories rather than political positions.

Not everyone will want to share everything. In some countries, it might be dangerous for them to share certain things. In some countries, political dissent has a heavy cost, and dissenting political opinions may be criminal offenses, even shared in a casual conversation. In such countries, it is much harder to engage with people about alternative political narratives. As a result, do not push someone to share political views, and if someone does share them with you, don't share any of this information with another local. In other words, we can ask, but we should also feel comfortable when people choose not to answer.

Hear the Opposing Narrative

Most travelers come to Jerusalem with an agenda already in mind, and they choose whom to speak with and what narratives to engage with based on that agenda. They are not looking for narratives that challenge their worldview—quite the opposite. They engage with people who will confirm their beliefs—whether they believe Israel is right and the Palestinians are wrong or vice versa.

To address this problem, Scott and I decided that for each of MEJDI's tours, we would start hiring both an Israeli guide and a Palestinian guide to lead the tour together. Now, for our tours, the two guides lead as partners, going to both traditional sites (like the Dome of the Rock, the Western Wall, and the Church of the Holy Sepulchre) and off-the-beaten-path sites (like the Separation Barrier, Palestinian refugee camps, and Israeli settlements). At each site, participants hear from both an Israeli Jew and a Palestinian Christian or Muslim. Participants get to hear different perspectives and stories about how each guide sees the site. Sometimes the stories complement each other, but in many cases the stories conflict—and that is OK.

In the beginning, I remember being asked, "Aren't you afraid that your guides will fight with each other? Won't that make the participants feel awkward?" Surprisingly, this has not been the case. We hire guides who believe in our mission and who are not there to prove that their side is right and the other side wrong. Instead, they consider the tour a learning opportunity and are committed to having a conversation with one another.

That said, we do not make our tours all about politics. We take a holistic approach, discussing history, archaeology, art, religion, poetry, politics, and culture. Amazingly, this approach has helped us build a community of tour guides from both sides. It has also led to a profound realization: on many topics—such as theology, archaeology, and art—the battle lines are not always Israeli versus Palestinian. We've discovered, for example, that the guides often debate Jericho's archaeological dating or where to find the best hummus in Jerusalem—topics that have nothing to do with their religious or ethnic backgrounds. One pair of our guides are in total agreement on their love of Lorde's music, and our tour groups will hear about it at some point during the tour. Their professional and individual identities often transcend national identity.

We also try to highlight the diversity within communities. I recently joined two of our tour guides, Yuval and Husam, while they were leading a tour in Jerusalem. Throughout the tour, Husam (the Palestinian guide) and I found that we (the two Palestinians) disagreed with each other more than we disagreed with the Israeli guide! When we were outside the Holy Sepulchre, Husam gave a passionate speech about the church and how in Palestinian Christian tradition, this was the site of the Crucifixion and Resurrection of Jesus Christ. In his view, other sites claiming to be the location of the Crucifixion disrespected the tradition and the archaeological findings.

Husam's view stems from the fact that he grew up a Muslim but went to a Catholic school. I grew up a Muslim too but went to a Protestant Bible college, where I learned a different perspective. So I disagreed with Husam's analysis. I argued that there is no conclusive evidence that the Holy Sepulchre is the site of the Crucifixion. I pointed out that the other possible sites for the Crucifixion, such as the Garden Tomb in Jerusalem, are equally valid. Ironically, instead of an Israeli Jew and Palestinian Muslim arguing about politics, two Palestinians from a Muslim background were arguing passionately about where Jesus was crucified, something that doesn't even fit with Islamic theology!

For our travelers (who were mostly Christians), this was an experience they didn't expect. They were touched by Husam's defense of Catholic sites in Jerusalem and by my defense of the Protestant narrative. But the argument between two Palestinians about the importance of Christian holy sites didn't fit into any narrative they had heard about Palestinians. They didn't know that many Palestinian Muslims attend Christian schools. They had come to hear the Israeli and Palestinian narratives, but they discovered that each of our communities has many narratives.

Practice Extreme Patience

I've mentioned that we should seek out and hear the opposing narrative. But I'm often asked: What about Israeli settlers or religious radicals? What about Palestinian extremists? Should we listen to them?

I often respond by telling the story of Daryl Davis. Daryl is one of my heroes. An African American from Chicago, Daryl taught me to expand my understanding of peacemaking. We all have red lines we don't cross—those people we just won't listen to. But by listening to Ku Klux Klan members as a black man, Daryl has persuaded more than 200 Klan members to leave the organization.

When I met Daryl, he started by telling me how he had met with a state leader in the Klan. The Klan leader came to his office and immediately started lecturing him on how black people are inferior, how blacks scam the government to get welfare, and how black people are lazy. He told Daryl that black people are criminals; he even said that black people's brains are smaller.

"Most people would have stopped him there and started arguing with him as soon as he started speaking. I didn't. I let him say everything he wanted. My willingness to listen surprised him," Daryl told me.

"But weren't you offended?" I asked. Daryl shrugged. "Sure, these things were offensive. But I wasn't offended. They didn't know me, or my life." The Klan member had never spent any time in an African American community. As Daryl explained, these lies about African Americans only showed ignorance.

Amazingly, Daryl let the Klan leader carry on his monologue for two hours! Then, after the Klan leader had said his piece, Daryl began engaging with him. He spoke without showing anger, raising his voice, or being condescending. He said, "I've never been in prison, I've always worked, and I've never been on welfare; and while I've never measured my head, I am pretty sure my brain is not smaller than others'." And for the first time in his life, the KKK leader was willing to hear what an African American man had to say. After that, Daryl and the Klan leader kept meeting, and over time they became friends.

One day, the Klan leader showed up at Daryl's office with his robe, swastikas, and other KKK paraphernalia. But he wasn't there to make trouble. Instead, he handed the gear over to Daryl. "It's yours to keep," the Klan leader told him, and said Daryl could burn it or keep it for educational purposes. He also told Daryl that he had decided to shut down his Ku Klux Klan chapter!

What can we learn from Daryl? Dealing with extreme ideologies takes extreme patience; it takes a lot of restraint to remain calm as we hear offensive things. That is why to me, Daryl Davis models the essence of peacemaking. By listening, Daryl persuaded the Klan leader to listen to him, respect him, and consider his ideas.

It is important to engage with people—even people who have extreme ideologies. Listening does not mean we accept or condone radical views. But we must differentiate the person from his or her extreme ideology. Daryl understood that reconciliation only comes though turning an enemy into a friend—and that requires listening to and showing respect for the other person.

Listening is an essential skill to learn as we travel. We shouldn't be preparing our responses to every offensive comment we hear. Instead, we should try to listen, understand, and then engage in a respectful conversation. No one reconsiders their views by being disrespected or yelled at.

We often worry about having the right answer to every comment or question, but most of the time, having a good argument is less important than how you treat people. People are less likely to listen to our opinions if we are not willing to listen to theirs. Daryl understood that listening is one of the most important tools at a peacemaker's disposal. He crossed lines even I was not willing to cross for many years—and his bravery and humility have saved both the men who were lost in their hateful ideology and those they might have hurt with their violence. While not all of us will be faced with the chance to speak with a KKK member, we will all meet people we disagree with. As a result, we can all practice patience and listen before we engage.

Discover the Invisible Stories

Egypt has a special place in my heart. Growing up, I spent every summer there visiting family. Yet when I was 26 years old, despite having been there dozens of times, I realized that I didn't actually know that much about Egypt. I knew my family, my friends and the neighborhoods they lived in. But I didn't know much about the area's history and the many minority groups in Egypt. I had never met a Christian Egyptian, even though there are over 10 million. I was no different than most of the tourists who visit Egypt for its archaeology and history—I had my familiar routine, and I stuck to what I knew.

Most tours and tourists in Egypt similarly stick to a familiar itinerary, ignoring the richness of Egypt's cultures and communities. It is true that there are many challenges if travel agencies want to go beyond the classic travel itineraries: tour operators are required to send every group itinerary to the Tourism Police, where an officer decides what should be removed from the planned schedule. The government also decides whether a police officer should join the tour for monitoring and security purposes. Moreover, the government removes from the itinerary most activities that allow travelers to meet with regular Egyptians because of security concerns. Yet, there can be a balance between security and allowing travelers to truly experience Egypt.

When I went back to Cairo, I knew that I wanted to connect with the unheard voices in Egypt. After all, Egypt isn't only the land of ancient pharaohs: it is also the land of storytellers, theater, cinema, music, and art; it is the humor and film capital of the Middle East, famous as the place where you can't be bored.

To tap into this rich culture, I decided to connect with the Christian community. On one of the trips I organized right after the 2011 revolution, I took travelers to Kasr El Dobara church in Tahrir Square in Cairo—the largest evangelical church in the Middle East. At the time, Sunday prayer services were attracting upwards of 7,000 Egyptian Christians.

Our American tourists never could have imagined such a large Christian community in the Middle East—despite there being an evangelical megachurch located in the heart of Cairo, in the bustling Tahrir Square. Following prayers, we met with the pastor. Since Tahrir Square served as the epicenter of the 2011 revolution, one of the tourists asked the pastor, "What did you do when the revolution was happening just outside your building?" The pastor replied that the church had opened its doors to the protesters. "Anyone who needed medical aid, water, or shelter at the time, we would try and help. We would go and clean up debris. We are a church, and the point of the church is to serve the people in need," he said.

In the United States, we hear a lot about conflicts between Christians and Muslims in the Middle East. So, it was important to hear different voices speak about the Muslim-Christian relationship in Egypt. We met with the Arab West Report, a nonprofit organization that promotes Muslim-Christian understanding. The organization tracks news reports of conflicts between Muslims and Christians in Egypt, then researches the facts. Most of the time, they end up discovering that the conflict had nothing to do with someone being a Christian or a Muslim but was about local issues between neighbors or tribes. But if the media (Egyptian or foreign) get their hands on a story that involves fighting between a Muslim and a Christian, they will often frame the conflict in religious terms. The Arab West Report challenges and disputes this narrative.

These stories don't negate the very real challenges faced by the Christian community in Egypt (challenges that include terror attacks on churches, a problem that has plagued Egypt in the last few years). We met with groups that talked about the attacks from radicals, and we learned about interfaith responses in which Muslims and Christians created human chains around "the others" to protect them while they were praying.

We also reached out to Muslim leaders, including a young Salafi activist. Salafism is a conservative Muslim movement. I was amazed that not only was he willing to meet with our group, but he offered to host us for lunch. He was excited that this group of 25 evangelical Christians from Washington, DC, wanted to hear from him and understand his worldview. When we arrived at the man's house, his wife walked in, dressed from head to toe in a niqab, in which you could only see her eyes.

As she prepared lunch for the group, the American tourists gave each other side glances and whispered to each other. One of the Americans finally spoke up, addressing the woman's husband. "Why does she wear the burqa [niqab]?"

Before the husband could reply, the woman looked at the man and warmly answered in fluent English, "I speak English, and it's OK, you can talk to me." This was not expected. The tourists were surprised.

In the Western mainstream narrative, any woman who wears a niqab must be deeply oppressed and allowed to speak only with the permission of her husband. But, contrary to that narrative, this woman was well-educated and had a voice as powerful as her husband's. It was the first time the tourists had ever spoken to a woman wearing a niqab.

The woman's response was a surprise welcomed by everyone. The tourists asked her some tough questions: "Why are you wearing this? What's the story behind it?" She responded by explaining that she wore the niqab because it was her choice, it seemed to her like a form of worship pleasing to God, and because it was a protest against the government's oppression and imprisonment of Salafis. She said that she liked the challenge that the niqab presented. Because she wore a niqab, she said, people made assumptions about her, and she enjoyed overturning those assumptions. She said that wearing it stripped away all the things she would normally use to prove her social worth: the niqab hid her makeup, her hair, her expensive clothes. Wearing the niqab, she had nothing but the force of her words and her personality—so she had to work extra-hard to speak up and assert herself. She hoped that in this way, people would judge her based on who she was as a person, not what she looked like. It was quite an interesting and unusual perspective!

The meeting with this family became one of the highlights of the trip, because it created an opportunity for a conversation. The conservative Muslim couple was curious about the Americans, wanted to hear the tourists' views on Islam and Egypt, and asked questions about Christianity. And even though the Americans and Egyptians didn't always agree politically, the conversation was friendly, constructive, and respectful. Many of the travelers walked away from their discussion with the niqab-wearing woman still not agreeing with her clothing choice, but they admitted the conversation had changed the way they viewed the women who wear the niqab.

Overall, Egypt is a diverse and culturally rich country, and the only way to explore that diversity is by meeting the people who don't fit within the main narrative of the destination. Having these interactions changed how the tourists felt about Egypt, and this change of heart in many cases led to changes in behavior. After returning to the United States, many of the travelers became more active on issues relating to the Middle East. One couple began helping refugees in DC; they decided to meet a refugee couple every week, help their children with homework, and share meals together.

I don't believe this personal growth would have been possible if all they had seen in Egypt was the pyramids, the Sphinx, and the temples at Luxor. They still visited these sites and got many Instagram-worthy photos. But if they had not challenged themselves to look beyond these activities, their hearts would not have been opened by the stories of the diverse people in the country.

Toward a More Inclusive Travel Experience

A few years back, I participated in an accelerator program run by a large travel company. There, a travel expert told me that telling multiple narratives and amplifying unknown stories didn't work outside of conflict areas like Israel and Palestine. Happily, he was wrong.

Highlighting diversity is the heart of travel. So when you plan your next vacation, get off the beaten path and contribute to making the narratives you hear more inclusive by trying a few simple exercises:

- Consider what stories might be silenced by your guidebook, missing from travel blog top-10 lists, or left off of mass-market tour itineraries.

- Remind yourself that you are an ambassador, engaged in cultural exchange.

- Ask locals questions. Don't just ask them their positions on politics or religion. Instead, ask them to tell you their story. Consider the diversity that exists *within* the religious or ethnic community you are visiting, and find ways to experience these different perspectives. Ask yourself, "Who is my 'other'?" (Muslims? Christians? Israelis? Palestinians? Republicans? Democrats?), and challenge yourself to share a meal with them or listen to their perspective. When listening, practice extreme patience, and treat others with kindness (even if you don't respect their opinions).

- Revise your itinerary so that it reflects a value on people, not just places and things.

Ibn Battuta, an Arab traveler who lived in the 14th century, said, "Travel makes you speechless, but then it turns you into a storyteller." The stories we can encounter on our travels will impact us and even render us speechless. However, those stories will remain with us forever. When we talk about our travels, it's these stories that we are likely to share. When I travel, I search for stories that will touch my heart. My understanding of exploration is that it's about seeking the untold stories that might surprise me, shock me, and at times even pain me. But I always ask myself when I travel, "Am I coming back with new stories to tell?" If not, then I haven't really traveled.

CHAPTER 5

HOW TO MEET PEOPLE
WHILE TRAVELING

I'M AN EXTROVERT. People often joke that I will talk to anything that moves. But even for someone like me, it's not always easy to connect with people from an entirely different country and culture, where social etiquette and language can dramatically diverge from your own.

Once, I visited Stockholm for a few days. As an extrovert and not knowing anyone in the country, I wanted to get to know the locals. So, I went to a pub for happy hour, which usually is a great way to meet people and hear their stories. This time, however, I struggled. Every time I tried to strike up a conversation with someone, I'd receive a short, curt answer.

My attempts at starting conversations being a failure, I took a boat tour of the Stockholm archipelago. On the boat, I noticed an older gentleman traveling alone and asked him where he was from. It turned out he was a German tourist taking a few days off from work. We bonded over a common love of football and ended up meeting multiple times in the next few days to travel around the city, explore the culture, and sample the cuisine. Honestly, he saved my trip and made it so much more fun!

Travel helps us to connect not only to people and cultures of the countries we visit, but also to other travelers. While traveling, I have met with thousands of people from all over the world and learned about their countries, their cultures, and their histories.

Putting ourselves out there, saying hello, and asking questions is not always easy. But it is one of the best ways to open up a conversation. People don't always respond, and that's OK. You can always try connecting with other travelers.

An easy and nonthreatening way to start a conversation is to ask questions of people with whom you are already going to be in contact, like the bartender or the waiter at a restaurant. Smaller local restaurants and bars with less traffic are easier for starting such conversations—and in some cases, these conversations can lead to the bartender introducing you to other local patrons. Talking to a taxi driver or a bored shopkeeper can also lead to interesting conversations. These are all people who can give you insider knowledge about your destination and great recommendations. The rewards of such small conversations can thus be incredible!

When I was in Kazan, Russia, I remember having one of those conversations with a local, who suggested that I visit Bulgar (which is a two-to-three-hour drive from Kazan). It turned out that very few tourists in Kazan traveled to Bulgar, but the city was very beautiful, with a wonderful history and architecture.

My friend Phil described a time when his willingness to connect with locals paid off. He was traveling to Australia and had a stopover in Fiji. He decided to visit a beach—but since it was a site catering to couples on honeymoon, he looked for other people to connect with. It turned out a local fisherman was also on the beach, and they struck up a conversation. The fisherman asked if Phil wanted to go fishing with him. Phil happily agreed.

But what Phil didn't know was that "by fishing, he meant I'd go out on the boat with him, then jump in the water and try to scare fish into his net. We ended up catching only about 10 fish in his gigantic net, which we immediately cooked over a tiny makeshift fire back on the beach. To this day, the best fish I've ever tasted!" After eating, the fisherman invited Phil to visit his village. On the way, they passed a tiny channel, and the fisherman joked that it was where his ancestors used to hide, to ambush settlers. "I nervously asked, 'But that was the old days, right?'"

The man showed Phil his humble home—a corrugated metal roof with dirt floors. He also proudly showed off his prized record collection, which was mostly Engelbert Humperdinck records! They ended up drinking kava together with the village elders in an old temple. Overall, Phil told me, "Joe [the fisherman] was fantastic—I couldn't have asked for a better day. I'm pretty glad I accepted his offer to help him fish!"

For me, this is what travel is all about: a meeting of two cultures, differences, and people who would never have met otherwise.

Be Cautious, but Stay Open

So what things should we consider when trying to meet locals? I asked my friend Katie over lunch about her experience traveling solo while considering safety. Katie is a traveler whom I met in Jerusalem 10 years ago. She told me about her trip to India. She was warned by many people about the challenges she would face as a woman, especially taking long-distance trains. When she booked her train from Rishikesh to Varanasi, she was tense and worried about strangers who would be sharing her cabin for the 19-hour ride. On top of that, she was recovering from dengue fever and was still feeling exhausted.

As she walked into her cabin, she was relieved to see that it was a couple and their two children who would be sharing the cabin with her. Quickly, a conversation started. The mother encouraged her 10-year-old daughter to practice English with Katie. She then asked Katie if she had ever met a Sikh person and pointed to her husband, a Sikh who wore a turban.

The woman shared with Katie stories about her life and family, and had many questions about Katie's life and experiences in India. Halfway through Katie's 19-hour trip, the family arrived at their destination. Before exiting the train, the woman took off her bracelet and gave it to Katie as a gift.

The family was replaced by two men: a younger man who was fresh out of college and an older man who didn't speak any English. It didn't take long before Katie and the men began discussing a newspaper the older man was reading. The conversation moved to politics and the Hindi language, and Katie shared with them her experiences traveling in India.

Each time the tea cart passed by their cabin, the old man bought all of them tea. When the tea cart wasn't around, he went to the café in the train to buy more. However, each time he bought tea in the café, he brought back tea only for himself and the other man.

The younger man explained that when they bought the tea from the cart, they could see the man pouring the water, and Katie could be assured that no one added any substance to the tea. But when the older man bought tea from the train's café, she couldn't see that the older man hadn't added anything to her tea on his way back from the café. "He is not being mean by not buying you tea from the café. He is just making sure you don't feel pressured to drink a tea you didn't see poured in front of you," the young man explained.

"We are all cautious with these things," the younger man continued. "It's not just because you are a tourist. There are criminals everywhere, and they would do it to me too." However, the younger man said that he trusted the older man and was willing to drink the tea that the older man brought from the café.

He also shared a story about a friend of his, an Indian man who had been drugged by a fellow traveler who offered him tea on the train. The friend woke up at a train station a few hours later, and all of his belongings were gone.

Being cautious is important, and making safety precautions is not something to take lightly. However, we should distinguish between being cautious and being judgmental and disconnected. India is a friendly country, and judging 1.3 billion people by the actions of a few criminals is absurd.

On one of the train stops, Katie got off to buy something from the station, assuming there was enough time. As she stood in line, however, someone poked her shoulder. She looked back and it was the young man. "You will miss the train!" he said. Katie hadn't noticed that it had already started to move. The young man had gotten off the train just to find her, risking that he might miss the train too. The two of them sprinted to the train and climbed back onto it.

By confronting her fear and misinformation she had received about India, Katie was able to experience a beautiful side of India that many miss. Conflicts erupt all over the world due to ignorance and fear. However, Katie took the peacemaker path in her travels by overcoming her fear and setting an example that other travelers can use as they pursue peacemaking through travel.

While traveling, you will encounter people who put your needs before their own and who will show you extreme generosity, despite the fact that often they have very little. You will meet people like this young man, who had risked missing the train just so he could help a stranger. I once was told that if we give people a chance, they are likely to surprise us with their hospitality, kindness, and compassion.

Get Out of Big Cities

You'd assume that it would be easier to meet people in bigger cities. There are more people there, and yet I find it harder to connect with locals and meet people in big cities than in smaller, less touristy places. Cities like Barcelona, London, and Paris have millions of residents. People are busy, crime rates are higher, and most people are cautious—making them sometimes more brusque and impatient with travelers.

So, when I travel, I always look for the less touristy, smaller cities, towns, and villages. When I visited Russia, I wanted to see Moscow. It was a fascinating city to visit, and the people there were very friendly. But it was Samara—not a popular destination for most travelers visiting Russia—that made me fall in love with the country. It was in Samara that I randomly met with Artum after a World Cup football match. After a few minutes of conversation, he invited me and three other tourists to his village.

You may ask yourself what there is to do in a tiny village. But many small towns have beautiful sites to visit, even if they are not Instagram famous. They are also great for building relationships and experiencing authentic local culture. Artum, for instance, introduced us to his mother and grandfather. He took us for a walk in his village, where we stumbled on an impressive domed structure and tower built from red bricks—a church bombed during the Russian Civil War. When we walked inside, I looked up at the broken and crumbling dome. I was amazed. Four icon paintings looked to be in perfect condition. I could see the details of the faces, and the colors were still vibrant. If you stayed silent long enough, it was easy to imagine yourself sitting in this church 100 years ago, listening to the hymns and sermons.

When we arrived back at the house, we chopped some firewood and pumped water from a tank outside the house into the kitchen. I felt like I was in a different world. Then we had a Russian barbecue, and our host brought out some homemade moonshine. We played Russian music, danced, and shared stories from our cultures and lives. Time passed so quickly that by the time we decided to leave, the sun was coming up.

I never imagined that a random lunch with a stranger would lead to the best night I experienced in Russia. Samara is rarely on people's travel bucket list, but for me it was an experience that rivaled Moscow. So next time you're visiting a destination, find a small town to explore. Head to the village plaza, get a coffee or grab lunch at a local café, visit the local park, or visit a temple in the area. You can even just ask a local, "What should I see in your town?" In this way, you'll experience a whole other side of life that most tourists miss.

Choose Human Interaction over Technology

We are more connected today than ever before, due to techno-logical developments. We can communicate with almost anyone instantly, regardless of distance. Yet despite these technological advancements, many people continue to feel lonely and iso-lated, because it is easier to sustain shallow social media rela-tionships than to have difficult, real-life relationships. It also has become easier to ask Google for travel advice, instead of asking our friends or locals for recommendations.

Technology provides us with a myriad of positive benefits, but it's one of the biggest barriers we face meeting fellow travel-ers and locals. We are so hooked to our phones that we are less likely to connect with the environment around us. We no longer ask questions or ask for directions—moments that offer wonder-ful openings and opportunities for connecting with strangers. We can end up traveling the whole world without speaking to anyone.

We live in a reality where technology has convinced some of us that we don't need other people. I also face these challenges. I know it would be much easier to check information on my phone than to talk to strangers. But I push myself to rely less on my phone—especially while traveling—and to be present to seize the moment. I look for opportunities to consult and connect with locals. I go out of my way to ask for suggestions: Which pubs do they go to? Which events do they attend? And where can I join a soccer match? When I am at a store, I avoid self-checkout machines. Relying less on technology and more on people has opened me up to a whole world of connections I would not have had otherwise.

Get Lost!

I had just landed in Tokyo, exhausted after a 14-hour flight from Washington, DC. On my way from the airport to the city, I tiredly observed the tall buildings and bright lights from the car window. I was taken aback by how similar Tokyo was to New York City; the traffic and the scores of people on the streets left me nostalgic for previous trips to the Big Apple.

When I arrived at my hotel, I freshened up and dropped by the reception desk to ask for suggestions on where I should go. They recommended city center areas like Shibuya and Harajuku, and I set off. However, on the way I ended up taking the wrong train, headed in the opposite direction. By the time I realized my mistake, I was speeding toward the outskirts of the city.

I got off at the next stop and faced a decision: should I turn around and head back to the city center or explore this unfamiliar neighborhood? Since it was late and I was hungry, I decided to find a restaurant. But by now it was around 10 p.m., and not much was open; the whole town seemed closed for business.

Suddenly I saw a door with a blinking neon sign, flashing on and off in Japanese characters. I thought perhaps it was a pub, so I swung the door open and walked in.

What I saw was remarkable.

The place had not been renovated for decades. It had a wooden bar and stools and small tables with vintage brown leather seats. The background of the bar had sliding cabinets where the drinks were stored. I felt I had traveled back in time. There were only a handful of customers—and the youngest looked to be in his 60s.

I sat down and ordered a drink. No one spoke English, but the bartender was a friendly older woman who spoiled me with her smiling, which helped me feel welcomed and comfortable.

A few minutes later, two of the customers grabbed microphones, and TV screens lit up behind the bar. I realized suddenly that I had discovered a karaoke bar on the outskirts of Tokyo, and the party was just getting started. They played what I believe were old Japanese folk songs. One of the first singers was probably 75 years old. He had a rough, deep voice.

They took their karaoke very seriously. When I tried to order another drink while the man was singing, I was told to wait. No one spoke or made any distractions while others were singing.

As I was sipping on my sake and admiring the singers happily belting out Japanese songs, one of the men looked at me with a smile and passed me a mic. "Oh," I said, a bit startled. "I don't speak Japanese, and I don't think I can sing. You probably don't want me to sing. When you hear my voice, you will understand."

They obviously didn't understand me, because they didn't speak a word of English. However, it turned out they actually had English songs on their karaoke playlist. As I stood there confused about how to even communicate, "Hey Jude," by the Beatles, started blaring from the speakers. They must have assumed that if they knew who the Beatles were, I must know too—and they were right!

I have never been given such a warm ovation for my singing; usually my friends quickly demand that I stop if I try to serenade them. Now I was in Japan, and not only did they cheer for me, but they encouraged me to keep singing, again and again.

The manager said something in Japanese to everyone and then walked through a door at the back of the bar. She came out with a rice hat and a long, white-striped jacket (which I was told later by friends is common dress for farmers). They dressed me in the farmer outfit, and we continued to sing until the end of the night. It was way past midnight by the time the party stopped.

I'll never forget that night, which taught me an important lesson: I shouldn't plan my every move. I should allow myself to get lost—albeit while taking safety precautions. Allowing ourselves unstructured time when we can let ourselves wander is immensely valuable, because sometimes strict schedules and itineraries prevent us from exploring. We should be open to letting go sometimes and allowing ourselves to live in the moment, even if that means missing out on more famous tourist sites. In the end, it is often these unstructured moments that can lead you to some of the most amazing people and places.

Slow Down

Growing up in Jerusalem, a popular tour destination for visitors to the Holy Land, I was always fascinated by tourists. As a kid, I went to Al-Aqsa School in Jerusalem—named after the Al-Aqsa Mosque. I went to kindergarten and summer camps held in the mosque compound, and on the way to and from school I passed many tourists. Each time, I would excitedly say, "Hello!" and try to catch their attention. Some of them would approach me, wait for my smile to widen, and then snap a photo. I would excitedly pose for them; I initially loved the attention.

Soon after they snapped the photo, however, their tour guide would typically intervene and tell them to keep moving. Even when they were alone, they would usually snap the photo, say thank you, and then move on. I hated that. I felt objectified. I wanted to speak to them, although I didn't have the English to hold a conversation. Still, they could have spent an extra minute or two speaking with me. But they had plans and places to go, more sites to see, and more people and places to take photos of.

Many travelers don't get to meet locals because they are in a hurry to get to their next planned activity. But we don't engage with people when we are racing from site to site, checking off a list of what we are expected to see. Often, travelers may not even like or care about the sites; they go because someone deemed the sites important in a guidebook.

But if you take the time and notice what's happening around you, you're more likely to meet locals and engage with them. You meet people when you slow down, observe what others are doing, and listen to what they are talking about. And by slowing down, you see and learn a lot more about the place you're visiting.

There's one core struggle I've noticed when I help travelers design their itineraries: overscheduling. They want to see everything. But at some point, when you plan too much, you don't give yourself the time to enjoy anything. Travelers are exhausted by the end of the trip and feel like they need a vacation from their vacation when they return home.

They also miss the beauty of the sites they're visiting, because they are checking the time and making sure they don't miss the next site. So instead of appreciating the moment, they obsess about making sure the next moment happens on schedule.

We need to learn to value the quality of our travel more than the quantity of travel. I don't care how many countries and cities you've visited, or how many sites you've seen in each country. Collecting passport stamps, checking off lists, and collecting selfies is no way to travel—and it's one of the worst trends in the travel industry.

Slow down, see fewer things, but truly experience them! Then you will notice that the people around you are open, and you'll find opportunities to connect with the people and places you visit.

Find Activities You Can Join

Just as travel shouldn't be about lists and rushing around, traveling shouldn't be a spectator sport. No one benefits from your being a passive consumer of culture. Therefore, I encourage travelers to get off the sidelines and get involved.

The easiest activities to join, where I've found most locals welcome travelers, are sports-related activities. While traveling in Cuba, Argentina, Brazil, Tunisia, Vietnam, Egypt, Russia, Cambodia, Ireland, and many other countries, I have always found a way to join a soccer match. Almost any time I pass a group of people playing soccer on the street, I try to stop and play with them for a few minutes. I've asked to join a match at least a hundred times during my travels, and only once was I told no.

Joining a sports activity can be a great way to meet locals. Afterward, you can talk about the match, the sport, and your favorite teams, and often the group will go out for a meal or drinks.

On my last trip to Vietnam, I was with two other travelers when we came across a family playing badminton in a park in Hanoi. We watched them for a few minutes, and then they stopped and invited us to play with them. For the next 20 minutes we joined the family in a fun badminton match. Obviously, we weren't as prepared as they were, and we lost miserably! But afterward we talked for a few minutes, took a group photo, and left. Even these brief experiences and interactions can be memorable.

If you are not a sports person, there are still many other activities you can join while traveling. One of my favorite activities is to take a cooking class. A cooking class can be a great way to learn about cultures and food, and hear fascinating stories— while also connecting with fellow travelers.

I prefer cooking classes that are hosted by local families over those offered by chefs at restaurants. Both can be good options, but visiting people's homes can give you a unique window into their daily lives. It's no wonder that Anthony Bourdain's show was a success. He understood that meeting people over a meal can be the best way to get to know them.

Travelers can also book experiences that help them connect with various organizations. Many places around the world offer classes aimed at connecting you to the local culture. In Vietnam, for instance, I've tried silver-making classes, a calligraphy class, and a home-visit lunch booked through a local company. Some of these experiences will particularly benefit those who prefer more stable, structured settings. Such activities can help more introverted travelers meet locals in small, personalized, timed, and safe settings.

There is also a great trend of travelers connecting with nonprofit organizations. These organizations are finding out that tourism is a productive avenue for spreading awareness about their work and beneficial for fundraising.

Overall, whether you join a sports match, connect with an NGO, take a music class, or learn how to cook local food, participating in activities while traveling can be fun, informative, and transformative. Activities help us connect with new people and help break down cultural barriers. But most important, they transform us from spectators to participants.

Is There a Simple Way to Meet People?

In the end, my most cherished travel moments are those times I have met people. But many of us are not sure how to do that. So is there a simple way to meet people?

The answer to this question will be different for each of us. But there are a few strategies you can use to increase the chances that you will make meaningful connections in the places you visit:

- Be cautious, but stay open. Consider safety, but don't let your fear stop you from reaching out to others.
- Talk to other travelers and explore together.
- Get out of big cities and explore smaller towns.
- Choose human interaction over technology. Put down the phone and start talking to people.
- Find areas where you can safely get lost and explore the world around you.
- Slow down, and build time to wander and interact with people into your schedule.
- Find activities that you can join.

By taking these types of steps, and by being curious and conscious about trying to meet locals, even the most introverted travelers can learn how to connect with others. It might simply start with greeting people, asking them questions, and seeing where the conversation goes. But ultimately, these are often the moments that lead to the travel experiences you'll cherish and remember for a lifetime. And most important, by connecting with people, we can help shift the culture of travel from valuing sites and photographs to valuing human life and intercultural exchange.

CHAPTER 6

AVOIDING "VOLUNTOURISM" AND "POVERTY TOURISM"

DURING COLLEGE I joined a small youth group in Jerusalem that focused on giving back to our society; we were all in our late teens and early 20s. There were elderly people in our community who were lonely and did not have caregivers to assist them; they didn't have any connections to the younger generation.

We decided that every week we would take a few hours to visit these people, spend time with them, clean their houses, and listen to their stories. I can still vividly picture their faces and the warmth I felt from them. I remember Georgette, a woman approaching her 80th birthday, with a charming and kind face. She lived in the Christian Quarter of the Old City in Jerusalem. I was a young boy from a Muslim family, visiting a Christian woman every week. But neither of us cared much about those labels. She didn't have any children, and I felt that she always treated me like a son. She didn't need much help with physical labor, but she enjoyed our visiting and spending time with her. I also loved listening to her stories about Jerusalem back in the 1940s and 1950s.

Later, we decided to start volunteering at a local orphanage and other institutions. This was my first encounter with volunteer work, and I have since realized that I benefited from these experiences even more than those I was helping. I learned from the wisdom of others. I witnessed the social problems and injustices in my community, and I was inspired by the resilience and strength of those who had very little. Volunteering taught me that my life should not be only about my own needs and desires. Therefore, I am a strong believer in volunteering and in organizations that provide people the opportunity to volunteer.

Volunteering versus Voluntourism

According to a 2014 NPR article, "More than 1.6 million volunteer tourists are spending about $2 billion each year."[1] This is a fast-growing trend, and while it is great that people are interested in doing good deeds while traveling, there are also significant concerns to address.

Mass tourism and volunteering do not partner well together. Instead, volunteering should be heavily regulated and needs to be supported by the entire community—not just a few tour operators who are benefiting from the volunteer industry.

In some countries, such as Cambodia, orphanage tourism has become a commercialized industry focused on creating maximum profit. According to a 2012 *Telegraph* report, UNICEF reported a significant increase in orphanages in Cambodia, from 153 to 269 between 2007 and 2012; however, only 21 of these were state run.[2] According to the *Guardian*, in 2017 the number grew to 406, housing over 16,500 children, yet 80 percent of them were not orphans.[3]

According to the NPR article, some of these orphanages were tourism scams, in which children at times were rented from their parents to show them off to tourists. In other cases, the orphanage directors kept the institution at a substandard level and the children in poor conditions in order to attract more donations. "Voluntourism" (short-term volunteering abroad, whose purpose is more tourism than community development) has become the cause of these children's suffering.

In light of these realities, it's important to ask questions before volunteering with an organization, especially if you're planning to work with children. First, do your research about the organization you want to volunteer with, and don't be enticed by slick marketing. Be wary of any organization that accepts tourists without requesting proof of your qualifications and expertise.

Second, seek references, and if possible reach out to others who have worked with that organization or volunteered there. This is important because it will also prepare you for the organization's work and for challenges you might face.

Third, make sure you are not stealing a local's job. Volunteering should be about helping the local community, not contributing to unemployment. Volunteers should be assisting local staff—not replacing them with free foreign labor.

Finally, be conscious of where your money is going and how it's being used by the organization. Kim Passy Yoseph, a colleague of mine at MEJDI Tours, volunteered in Ethiopia. She did her research and ended up volunteering at a hospital on the outskirts of Addis Ababa. The hospital had a disabled boys' orphanage, but not every volunteer had access to it. The hospital staff believed that short-term volunteers would create abandonment issues for the kids when the volunteers left. So, only long-term volunteers who had shown commitment were eventually introduced to the kids.

The local staff at the hospital also made each volunteer prove that he or she was there for work and not just for a fun adventure. In the first week, volunteers were tasked with cleaning the hospital and taking a language course; this was to assure the staff that volunteers genuinely cared about working at the hospital before they were assigned to a section.

Kim learned sign language and used the Amharic she had learned to translate between doctors and deaf patients. "I had to ditch the attitude that we are going there to change the world. My main job was really to make the lives of the Ethiopian employees a little easier. They worked over 10 hours a day," she said. Volunteers in that hospital were there to help local staff and not replace them. Other professional volunteers had also participated: a physiotherapist from England, for instance, didn't work directly with patients. Instead, she focused on increasing the capacity of the Ethiopian staff to conduct this particular kind of work.

We all have expertise and knowledge we can share with the world, and we can use these skills when we volunteer. There are great organizations out there with impressive volunteering projects. MovingWorlds, for instance, was founded by professionals who wanted to use their skills to assist organizations and social enterprises in areas where they might have a lack of either human resources or financial capacity. MovingWorlds connects professionals to these organizations and provides training to travelers to ensure that the outcome of their experiences matches their expectations.

People and Places is also a great organization.[4] They connect travelers to projects based on specific skills needed in real time. Like MovingWorlds, they expect volunteers to have experience in the field where they want to work, and they have a list of qualifications and expectations for each position. They are committed to not threatening local jobs, and the travelers pay the local organizations directly in country instead of paying People and Places, which demonstrates outstanding transparency. These local organizations are continuously vetted by People and Places to make sure that the funds are going to their intended purpose and that volunteers are fulfilling their mission without harming the local communities.

Volunteering Is Educational

When Kim finished her army service in Israel as a commander and a training officer, she subsequently decided to take some time off and volunteer. While many Israelis take a year after the army to travel and explore the world, Kim felt that she should focus on volunteering.

Kim was not new to volunteering. Living in Kochav Yair, on the outskirts of Tel Aviv, she realized that she had never met an Ethiopian Jew and decided to volunteer with an Ethiopian community that lived just a half hour away from her. Kim volunteered to help the community's youth scouts.

During this volunteer experience, her interest in Africa began taking shape. She decided to travel to the continent during her gap year before army service. She first traveled to Zimbabwe and volunteered for two months, and then headed to Ethiopia for another two months.

In Zimbabwe, she taught English to a group of teenagers. The classes included leadership training, civil and human rights issues, and world affairs. At the same time, she learned from the teens and their realities in Zimbabwe. She learned about extreme poverty and lack of opportunities that they faced.

During her time in Zimbabwe, Kim lived with a white Zimbabwean family that wasn't pleased with her decision to volunteer with the black community, and they continued to question her resolve to support their "enemy." The division between whites and blacks in Zimbabwe has a long and brutal history—rooted in the bloody legacy of colonization.

Former Zimbabwean President Robert Mugabe headed a land reform policy that redistributed thousands of farms owned by the white minority of Zimbabweans to black citizens. Mugabe viewed the land ownership by whites as a consequence of colonization and claimed that redistributing land would offer greater equality.

The family that Kim stayed with had lost their land under Mugabe's reforms. They questioned Kim's decision to come all the way from Israel to volunteer with a population they saw as their enemy. Kim was quickly compelled to learn about the country's history and engage in discussions with various groups to understand the multiplicity of narratives in the country.

However, her experience in Zimbabwe had an impact that hit closer to home; it reminded her of the situation between Israelis and Palestinians. She had also met people from various parts of the world who had come to Israel and Palestine to volunteer with Palestinians. She told me that she felt frustrated at one point when she met a group of travelers who were intending to join a peace march in Bethlehem but had no plans to visit Israeli communities. She didn't understand why someone would volunteer only on the Palestinian side. As an Israeli soldier, she viewed Palestinians as her enemy, and these volunteers were there to support her enemy.

"The white Zimbabwean family was mirroring my earlier thoughts, I realized," Kim explained to me. "Maybe the person that I think is an enemy, others don't see them this way."

She returned home with the belief that everyone is entitled to have a good life. "I realized that my life in Israel was much better than how many Palestinians live, especially in Gaza," she said. "Maybe, when I go back home and think about what's happening back in Israel, I could volunteer and help, because I knew Palestinians were having a difficult life. I was definitely less judgmental and more open-minded after this experience." Upon returning, Kim engaged with the Palestinian community, and that was what led to her work with MEJDI Tours. Her transformation had an effect on her family as well. Recently, I was invited to spend the evening with Kim and her extended family for Shabbat dinner, and in 2018, Kim arranged for me to travel to Russia for the World Cup with her brother and father (a former Israeli football player).

Kim's volunteering experience not only helped her to understand the conflict in Zimbabwe but also assisted her in reflecting on the conflict in her home country. She learned to be less judgmental, and today she works overseeing travel programs that bring Palestinians and Israelis together. She works side by side with Palestinian tour guides and Palestinian speakers, and has become a leader in educational travel in the Middle East.

Volunteering for Kim didn't end when she left Ethiopia. It has built bridges for her back home in Israel. She was able to connect with her own community much better because of her volunteering experience overseas. For her, volunteering wasn't a onetime thing but rather a lifestyle that would continue to shape her character and her relationships.

Poverty Tourism versus Social Justice Tours

I have been to Brazil a half dozen times, and each time I visit, I learn new narratives and new perspectives. I have learned about colonialism and how it has continued to impact Brazil today, I have learned about dictatorship in the country's history, and I have learned about the environmental issues of legal and illegal logging in the Amazon rainforest. However, nothing has affected me as much as learning about the poverty and violence in the country's favelas.

A few years ago, I visited São Paulo, the largest city in Brazil (a city that often appears on "Most Dangerous Cities in the World" lists), to try to learn more about the challenges that the city faces. I wanted to visit a favela but was cautious about taking a "favela tour" because quite a few of them were engaged in "poverty tourism."

I feel strongly that while it is important to engage with modern issues, we should also refuse to participate in poverty tourism and disaster tourism. What's the difference between responsible tourism and disaster or poverty tourism? In my experience, poverty tourism tends to consist of tourists visiting a poor area for a short time; traipsing through neighborhoods; and occasionally stopping to take photos of residents or pose for a few Instagram shots with poor African, Asian, or Latin American children. It doesn't employ locals; most of the income goes to external tour operators; and residents have no say in the route, stories, or outcome of the tours. I find this kind of tourism disrespectful and even disgusting, and I'm not willing to engage in it.

To avoid this kind of tourism, in Brazil I asked my friend Marina, who was working for an environmental NGO, if she knew someone from a favela in São Paulo. She quickly introduced me to her coworker Marcia Lica from Real Parque. Marcia was born in the interior of Brazil, in a city located in the Amazon region. She is the eldest of five girls. Her mother had her at 17 and was unable to raise her, forcing her to live with her grandmother for some time.

Searching for a better life, Marcia's mother and her husband decided to move to São Paulo. Marcia joined them in the favela Real Parque when she was 13. When she arrived, she quickly noticed that the conditions in her new home were worse than she could have imagined.

"I imagined that in São Paulo everything was beautiful: big houses, cars—just like we saw on TV," she told me. "When I arrived in Real Parque, I was scared; it was a pile of crammed wooden shacks, sewage, garbage, rats, cockroaches, and I still remember the terrible smell. There was no bathroom in our shack."

As she recalled, "When it was raining hard, the neighbor's sewage passed into our room. It was very stinky—an inhuman place. As a child, I had no idea that we were living in a situation that was not only representative of poverty, but also of misery and a violation of our rights," she said.

"The favela was very violent. Every day, there was a [dead] body on the street. Seeing the dead became almost normal for the residents. It just happened. Today I understand that what we saw was a war."

On our way to the favela, we passed through the Morumbi neighborhood—one of the nicest neighborhoods in Brazil, known for having the most expensive real estate in São Paulo. The reality of poverty in the favela is even more stark, because it's located near this neighborhood's luxurious mansions and businesses.

It took Marcia only two years to organize and become a leader in her community. Soon after she celebrated her 15th birthday, she was already organizing social justice initiatives. She became involved in educational and cultural projects for young women, such as helping them to read. When I asked her where a 15-year-old found the courage to become a social activist in such hard living conditions, she replied, "I believe our mothers taught us to be strong and to not conform to this reality of inequality, and to intervene to make things better through theater, dance, music, and protesting against the government." As she put it, she realized there was no other choice but to change the realities on the ground, and she refused to accept that this was what her community deserved.

As I walked through the favela, it didn't actually look that bad. The houses seemed decent. I didn't smell any sewage, and the school building had a nice classroom and a decent football court on the roof. This was when I was invited to play a soccer match with the kids in the neighborhood, and it was there where

I learned that some stereotypes are accurate: Brazilians are extremely talented at football!

Marcia told me that when she was 21 and in her third year of college, she was among the leaders in her community who challenged the city, a real estate company, and the police in order to protect her community. Some residents were displaced, and land was being set for confiscation to build a new road and develop real estate. The favela residents eventually won and even managed to organize an urbanization plan that led to the rebuilding of the favela. Now, they have decent housing, plumbing, electricity, and a functional sewage system.

But what excites Marcia the most about these changes is her hope that the next generation will now have the opportunity to step out of poverty and fulfill their dreams. "We started to have a generation—our children, nephews, and nieces—who already dream much bigger than we did because this generation isn't living the violence we experienced and the conditions we endured."

Despite the past and current challenges, Marcia loves the favela because it has become her home. She talks about her favela with passion. It's sometimes easy to forget that she is talking about an impoverished neighborhood, because she sees what most of us from the outside never get the opportunity to see.

"I like the people, the coexistence on the streets, the children playing on the blocks of the buildings. My neighbors know me and greet me every morning. If I'm sick or I need help, I know I'm not alone. Here everyone knows their neighbors and cares about each other. We have many challenges, but we are a community, which is something rare in a giant city like São Paulo," she told me.

"When I return from work and enter the favela, I feel safe. I know that I won't be robbed or raped. Sadly, my only fear in the favela is from the police."

This is unfortunately not the reality that most people think about when they hear the word *favela*. But people in the favela are not what you typically see in the media. As I walked through the neighborhood, I wasn't scared. The residents were welcoming, and many were happy that I was there.

I felt I was visiting a community that valued friendships and relationships. The stories of the favela Real Parque were stories of inspiration and overcoming—stories that should be told all over the world. Marcia's activities, which challenge the negative stereotypes about favelas, are inspiring.

"I feel better being in any favela in Brazil than any other place. I feel at home. If you come to visit us, come with respect, and learn about our lives," she said.

I asked Marcia what she thought about the favela tours that often run in São Paulo. As she explained, these tourists visit the favelas to get a good shot of poor children in the streets. These people do not respect the community members' privacy and disrespect the locals. Marcia said that no one in the world would allow someone into their home with a camera aimed and ready to take photos of their children, bathroom, and bedroom.

"We are not just characters for tourist photography; we have stories. Can you imagine if I walked into a wealthy neighborhood, took a picture of their daily lives, their kids, their homes, and then published the photos without permission?" Marcia said.

Travelers are still welcome, but they must engage with the community and ask permission to visit the favela. Travel agencies bringing tourists need to coordinate with community leaders and communicate with travelers regarding what's acceptable and what's not acceptable during the visit.

There also need to be clear benefits to the community from these tours. Families who host travelers should be reimbursed fairly. The profits should not go only to the travel agency. And gift handouts to poor children are not enough (and in fact often do a lot of harm to the community, which comes to associate foreigners with handouts).

Each community and person is complex and multidimensional—and everyone wants to be recognized for more than just the negative aspects of their lives. Unfortunately, too many tours in the favelas focus only on the negatives. Poverty, crime, and danger are the central topics for tour companies that package the favela tours as an "adventure" or "exploration" of a poor neighborhood, instead of an important educational opportunity.

When we visit a new place, we should look into what the local community wants us to learn about their neighborhoods, lives, and traditions. Residents in the Brazilian favelas do not want us to learn only about their suffering; they also want their stories of struggle and innovation to be heard. When we actually listen to the local people, that's when we begin to see them as human beings and break the stereotypes that simplify their complex lives into a caricature of poverty.

During my day with Marcia in the favela, I met artists, students, photographers, shopkeepers, social activists, and various other people. I did not listen to just one narrative; I listened to a variety of narratives and local stories. I was overwhelmed by the generosity of the locals there.

We were invited for a drink by almost every shopkeeper we passed. I had lunch with Marcia's family and met her sisters, nephews, nieces, and mother. At no point during my visit did I feel uncomfortable or unsafe. Marcia told me that this was because I was not there as an intruder. Instead, I was there as a guest.

Owing to my experience in the favela, I could never again think of a favela (or any other poor neighborhood) in a singular narrative that generalized the complex lives of the people there. Indeed, a place that raised a strong and inspirational leader like Marcia must have many positive lessons to offer the world.

My experience in the favela was different from poverty tourism, which doesn't have any respect for the travelers or the local communities. I remember visiting New Orleans a year after Hurricane Katrina and coming across an advertisement that offered tours "of Hurricane Katrina's most hit areas from the comfort of your air-conditioned bus." Basically, go and see the suffering of people who have lost their homes. Poverty tourism doesn't offer any true engagement with people and doesn't benefit anyone but the tour operator's profit.

So, if you find yourself on a social justice tour, ask the local operator a few questions, such as these:

- Will we meet with locals on this tour? Who are they?

- How do you cooperate with the local communities?

- How did you decide on how to build the route for this tour?

- How does the community benefit from the tour? Do you pay local guides and speakers?

- What is acceptable and what is not acceptable for us to do on the tour?

Consider Your Motives

You know that voluntourism has become a problem when the *Onion* runs stories like "6-Day Visit to Rural African Village Completely Changes Woman's Facebook Profile Picture,"[5] and Instagram has a parody account (@BarbieSavior) that uses dolls to re-create women's photos with African children, with the description "Jesus. Adventures. Africa. Two worlds. One love. Babies. Beauty. Not qualified. Called. 20 years young. It's not about me . . . but it kind of is."

Volunteering while traveling can be complicated. Many people ask me about traveling abroad to volunteer—where they should go and what kind of volunteering they should do. My first response is to ask whether they have volunteered in their own communities. Volunteering is not for everyone, but those interested in volunteering must be motivated by the desire to help others. It's hard to make a case for helping people living thousands of miles away if a person has not volunteered in his or her own community. Volunteering should be a way of life, not an "experience" on a tour.

If people see volunteering abroad as romanticized and a "fun activity," but view volunteering at home as boring or unnecessary, that is usually a red flag that their desire to volunteer is about them—not about the people they want to visit.

In 2017, I was invited to speak at a middle school in São Paulo about my educational work with Syrian refugees. After my presentation about the Syrian refugee crisis, in which I highlighted stories of the resilience and aspirations of Syrian kids, I found myself surrounded by dozens of 13- and 14-year-old children who were moved by the stories of these refugees.

Mari, a 13-year-old, walked up to me and said that she wanted to help Syrian refugees, but because she lived in Brazil, she wasn't able to. "But I want to help people in my own community. I will talk to my mother today about us volunteering in São Paulo," she said. I felt inspired by this young girl; despite her age, she had understood that my message wasn't about everyone traveling to Syria to help out—which is neither feasible nor sustainable. Instead, it was about helping in our own communities. Mari was a perfect example of where volunteering needs to start.

If you are interested in volunteering abroad, consider volunteering in your own city or country first; this way, you can learn about the essence of volunteering, deal with everyday challenges, and figure out what your skill sets are. Those who travel abroad to volunteer for the first time may end up facing unexpected issues in a new country.

Volunteering abroad is also often counterproductive. In Turkey, I met with Shannon, an Australian who had been living in Istanbul for a number of years. She sat on the board of a refugee community center in the city. As she explained, she got countless emails and calls from tourists hoping to volunteer at the center. Often, foreigners would call and ask to volunteer for a few hours or for one or two days. But as Shannon described, she rejected most of these inquiries, because the volunteer would create more work for the center. Providing an orientation to these volunteers was time-consuming for the staff and was not worth it, compared with the short amount of time the volunteers would be staying.

It is good for tourists to want to help, but short-term volunteering can be problematic and unsustainable. It provides a good feeling to the tourist, but it often fails to help the organization needing assistance. In some cases, it actually hurts the organization by taking up its time, focus, and resources.

Some experienced organizations, like Habitat for Humanity, have successfully designed programs that work for short-term travel; but the majority of organizations do not have such programs or expertise in place. I have heard numerous stories of people volunteering to build or reconstruct homes and schools, and the moment the volunteers went to bed, the locals stayed up all night fixing what the volunteers had done—because the volunteers had no real experience in construction and had no guidance or experts to help them. Some opportunistic tour operators taking advantage of well-intentioned travelers run "construction tours" to build houses or schools without proper preparation or collaboration with local communities, causing more harm than good.

Our motivation for volunteering must be something we examine within ourselves. We must ask ourselves why we are interested in volunteering while traveling. If travelers' motivation is to feel good about themselves, have more meaning in their life, or have a good time as part of a short-term volunteering experience, then they probably shouldn't do it. I encourage travelers to also ask themselves: Have I volunteered at home, or do I just want to volunteer somewhere "exotic"? What are my skills? If you have never worked with children or have no teaching experience, then teaching might not be the best option for you.

Volunteering should be less about the experiences of the traveler and more about the impact it will have on the community or organization receiving the volunteers. It's not an opportunity for an Instagram moment with refugees or poor children. (There's something wrong when the entire time that travelers are volunteering, they are just taking photos of themselves hugging children and uploading them on their social media.) If your main focus is *showing* people what you are volunteering, then your activities are more harmful than helpful.

Volunteering Should Empower Others

Volunteering shouldn't be about self-glorification or amplifying your voice, but rather about helping underprivileged communities amplify their voice. And there are a few constructive ways you can do that.

In 2014, I visited Zaatari camp in Jordan with the Red Crescent to help take photos of the organization's activities. As I walked around the bleak desert encampment—rows of white tents on a flat, hard, cracked desert plain—I took photos, talking with the refugees and gathering stories. It was around noon, and no less than 100 degrees outside, when I saw a child who couldn't have been older than four or five years old. He was frowning and walking toward me from a tent in the distance. As he got closer, a wide smile formed on his face.

I aimed my camera at him and took a photo, as his smile spread from ear to ear. When I approached to speak to him, I noticed what had prompted his wide grin: a piece of trash on the ground. That piece of trash was the only toy he had found to play with in the camp, and it made him so excited that he could hardly contain himself.

His name, he told me, was Ahmad. I asked him how long he had been in the camp. He bluntly replied, "Always." The camp had been established two years earlier, so that couldn't be possible, I thought. But then I realized that two years represented half of this child's life. He didn't remember what life was like the year before.

I ended up telling his story through photographs during presentations I did in the United States, Europe, and South America. He became a symbol for me of what being a refugee means. I wanted the world to understand the suffering of these refugee children.

However, one day, when I was speaking about Ahmad during one of my presentations, it dawned on me that I wasn't actually telling his story. I was telling my own story of how I had encountered him and what I felt he represented.

I decided it was important to create spaces where refugees could tell their own stories, through their own eyes, words, and camera lenses. I contacted *National Geographic*, and they agreed to help set up a photography camp in Jordan. The camp would teach the kids, who were about 13 to 14 years old, how to take their own photos and tell their own stories.

We set up the project as a collaboration between several famous photographers and some local Jordanians and Syrians. Each day, we worked with the kids, teaching them photography and editing skills. Then we sent them out with cameras so they could take pictures of their lives in the camp.

They were fast learners! When they showed us the photos they had taken around the camp, I was shocked by both the quality and the content. I had assumed that their photos would show the suffering, poverty, and pain they were experiencing in the camp. I was wrong. What the children deemed important was entirely different from what I had tried to say for them as an outsider. A lot of their photos were of family, friends, and each other. One of them took a picture of a pigeon on his hand, preparing to fly. These were messages of hope, emphasizing the importance of love, family, and relationships.

In the long run, the project helped empower the children to tell their stories. The children who participated in that project, now in college, still engage in different projects, speaking about their lives, their stories, and their photography (which has been exhibited in such venues as the Kennedy Center in Washington, DC, and published in *National Geographic* magazine). At times, they are paid to speak and spread awareness about Syrian refugees to groups visiting Jordan; this helps sustain their situation while they are paying for college or assisting their families.

Since I work in cultural education, after the photography workshop in Jordan, I also spoke with teachers in Brazil about these children's stories. The teachers expressed interest in arranging a recurring Skype session between Brazilian students and Syrian students in Jordan to practice English, learn about one another, and share their stories. These encounters were transformational because the kids realized that the world was bigger than what they could see. The Syrian teenagers were moved by the compassion and care that their Brazilian counterparts had for them.

This example should emphasize to travelers how important it is to not just come into a community, take pictures, and then share those people's stories. We should also be looking for sustainable ways to provide platforms for communities to tell their own stories. When we connect with a community, we should consider our own networks and abilities, and ask if there is a way we can use these resources to empower communities and help others amplify their voices.

Of course, we should speak about the people and stories we've encountered in our travels, but we should always be conscious of the fact that appointing ourselves as a spokesperson for a community is not always the most positive action to take—even if it's well-intentioned. We should always make it clear when we speak about another community that it is from our own perspective as a traveler; spending a week in a place does not make you an authority on that community.

Volunteering and Visiting Underprivileged Communities in a Constructive Way

I strongly believe in the value of volunteering. It has shaped my understanding of my own city in Jerusalem. There are very few things as fulfilling or educational as volunteering.

But volunteering and visiting underprivileged communities must be less about our own needs and fulfillment, and more about those we aim to help. As a result, here are a few tips I suggest that travelers consider to keep volunteering sustainable, responsible, and constructive:

- Don't volunteer abroad if you are not willing to do it at home in your own city or country.
- Evaluate your motives for wanting to volunteer or visit an underprivileged community.
- Choose long-term volunteer programs; approach short-term programs with caution.

- Be wary of any organization that accepts tourists without requesting proof of appropriate qualifications and expertise.

- Do your research about the organization you want to volunteer with. Know how the organization is using its money. (Do a web search or request its annual report, and see how much is going to actual programs and how much is being used for administration and overhead. In almost every country, organizations are required to release this information to maintain nonprofit status.)

- Don't take unpaid volunteer jobs that a local could be doing in a paid position.

- Don't visit or take tours through poor areas, spend a few hours taking photos, then leave. Evaluate why you want to go, and if you go, connect with local organizations you can engage with and support.

- Don't speak for others; empower others to speak for themselves.

- Ask how you can use your networks, talents, and resources to create (or support) platforms that empower locals.

It is extremely important that when volunteering, we follow the principle "First, do no harm." Gift handouts, visiting poor neighborhoods to take pictures with children, and constant turnovers of unqualified foreign labor can harm communities and deepen cultural misunderstanding.

As a result, if you volunteer abroad or visit a poor neighborhood, do so with care and reflection. There is nothing responsible about using privilege to patronize others, exacerbate inequalities, and rob people of their human dignity. Those we take photos of are people, not scenery. Whether volunteering or taking a tour, we must recognize our privilege and not use it to demean others, exacerbate inequalities, or rob people of their human dignity. Our own desires for attention, meaning, or self-satisfaction are not as important as the health and well-being of the communities we visit.

CHAPTER 7

OVERCOMING FEAR, STEREOTYPES, AND NEGATIVITY

TRAVEL IS NOT all roses and butterflies. Throughout my travels, I have come across people who treated me differently because of my skin color, my birthplace, or my beliefs.

During one of my trips to Paris, I went to catch up with some friends at one of the city's many wine bars. As the group began to disperse for the evening, I stepped outside the café, which was located right off the Seine, and stood there appreciating the beauty of the evening.

After a few minutes, an older French woman approached me and began speaking French. Not knowing French, I responded in English. She asked me what I was doing in France and where I was from. She then asked me if I spoke other languages. I told her I spoke Arabic—and she spat on me and walked away. I was in shock.

The interaction with that French woman was not the only incident like this that I've faced. I have many similar stories. I was yelled at by a white woman at a grocery store in New York

City, who demanded I keep at least three feet away from her while we stood in line to pay. I was questioned by a stranger in Washington, DC, because he thought I was trying to steal my own car (even though I clearly had keys for the car). I've been denied services because of my name and ethnicity all over the world. I have also been called derogatory terms like "towelhead."

This is part of the travel experience for me. Each of us experiences different kinds of attention and treatment when we travel. My white friends have different experiences than I do in Latin America or the Middle East, where I pass as a local. In many parts of the world, it can be difficult for a woman to travel alone without encountering sexist comments. As my friend Ellie will describe in Chapter 9 (dedicated to traveling as a female), women travelers face harassment, unwanted sexual advances, and derogatory treatment.

Moreover, each time we arrive at a new destination, we not only have to face the assumptions that others have about us—we have to face our own assumptions. And this can lead to some uncomfortable moments. So how do we, as travelers, begin to recognize and break down our own assumptions about others? And how do we respond to people who hold stereotypes about us?

Working in the travel industry means that I often hear offensive comments and ignorant statements. It becomes somewhat normal when you're meeting thousands of people—all of whom grew up with certain prejudices and many of whom know little about the destination they're visiting. I don't believe in judging them, arguing with them, or feeling superior to them. We are all more similar than we'd like to believe, and most of us are unaware of our prejudices. Instead of getting mad, it's important that we look at travel and travel companions as an educational opportunity.

During one of our tours in Israel and Palestine, one of the participants was an older man from the United States who held strong pro-Israeli views. One of his first comments after meeting me was "I don't understand why the Palestinians don't just pack up and leave to Jordan."

I decided not to fight him on his ideas. I let him speak his mind with the understanding that he clearly had a lot of stereotypes about this place. I just took a deep breath and braced myself for what I assumed was going to be some long days ahead.

On day five of the 10-day tour, this same man was sitting with me and another tour participant, who also had strong pro-Israeli views on the conflict. The man who I had assumed would lead me to an aching headache by the end of the tour said something that shocked me: "I think we need to figure out a way for Israelis and Palestinians to live together." My head turned in surprise. He continued, "Both groups deserve peace and security in this place."

My mind could hardly process what he had just said. "Five days ago, you said we Palestinians should pack up our belongings and leave," I said to him.

"Yes, but that was before I arrived on this tour and met Palestinians. Now, I have eaten with Palestinians and Israelis in their homes. I have heard stories from different sides. The situation is different than what I thought," he said.

I went through the same process when I first began traveling. The first time I visited the United States at 20 years old, I was excited. It was my first time getting a glimpse into this mysterious country that occupied our TV screens and imaginations in East Jerusalem. I had learned about the United States from cowboy movies and crime films. I thought the United States was one action movie, with guns and shootings!

Needless to say, my excitement was equally matched by my terror. But despite my fears, I made it through my first trip to Los Angeles unharmed and avoided any situations involving police, shootings, or grand theft auto.

I did learn very quickly, however, how different my culture was when I went to the mall. There, I tried to buy a gift for my mother; and when the salesman quoted me $90 for a stainless steel watch, I countered with a $30 offer, leaving the salesman stunned. My Middle Eastern haggling at the mall was not what he expected.

"We don't do that here," he responded. I retorted in the same way I would have in the Middle East: "Look. I will give you $50 for it. If you don't accept, then I'm leaving."

Again, his reply was a polite but confused reiteration of "I'm sorry, but I can't do that." I thought I knew exactly what I had to do to twist his arm into lowering the price: I walked out. But I realized that something was wrong when I didn't hear him call me back into the store with a more reasonable offer (as would have happened in a Middle Eastern market).

You don't buy anything in the Middle East without haggling down the price, and I had assumed the United States was no different. After all, US tourists who visit Jerusalem seem to be well adept at haggling in our markets. My newly acquired American friends told me later that haggling like this is not acceptable in department stores in the United States, and there was no way to get out of paying the advertised price for my mom's watch.

My second time visiting the United States, I was in Washington, DC. There was a small but powerful incident in DC that made me realize how much stereotypes become part of who we are—even if there's no reason for it. Some of these stereotypes are hidden until we are forced to encounter them.

On day, I visited a local mall, and I needed to use the bathroom. As I walked in, a black man wearing a black hat and hoodie walked in behind me. Right away, my mind went to the American movies I had watched growing up, which commonly painted all black characters as dangerous criminals. I panicked. I started shaking, and the only thing I could think about was if he was going to murder me or rob me. There was no reason for me to feel like this; I have never had a bad experience with an African American.

After the man finished his business and left without robbing or murdering me, I felt horrible. I couldn't understand why I had experienced that kind of reaction. I realized that I had just stereotyped this person solely based on his skin color. The man was just minding his own business, thankfully completely un- aware that I was battling a war in my mind until the moment he walked out. Fear is a horrible thing, especially when there's no real reason for it. I started to think: Why was I so afraid? Why did I stereotype this person?

It hit me who the culprit was: all of those American action movies I had consumed as a kid. They were the only knowledge I had of black people in the United States; I had had no other encounters with African Americans. It's astonishing how much media can influence our views of other people, skin colors, cul- tures, nationalities, genders, and ethnicities—even when we're not aware of it. Traveling to the United States thus made me aware of my stereotypes, and I began to think about how to counter them.

Many people who travel to Israel and Palestine most likely have the same stereotypes about me as a Palestinian. Just as my assumptions about the African American man were not fair, neither are theirs. I used to get angry at Israelis and foreigners who assumed I was dangerous solely because I am Palestinian. But then, how could I be angry at them, when I did the same thing to African Americans when traveling to the United States?

We are confronted with our own stereotypes when we travel and experience other cultures and worldviews. This kind of reali- zation cannot always be achieved through passive learning alone. Reading an article or watching a documentary can challenge your worldview, but nothing beats the self-transformation you experience by putting yourself in a situation where subtle smiles, laughter, and voices can challenge even your hardest convictions.

I have seen this in many countries around the world. Stereotypes and generalizations about those who are of different races, religions, classes, and ethnicities are common in every society. That is why I deeply believe that if you want to uncover and challenge your prejudices, it is important to travel.

About 12 years ago, I was invited to speak on a panel with Nobel Peace laureate Betty Williams, who told me a story about how she had battled stereotypes in Northern Ireland.

Williams described how much the conflict in Northern Ireland is intertwined with identity and everyday life. Catholic and Protestant children often don't understand that the world is bigger than their conflict.

As a result, Williams worked to bring Catholic and Protestant children together, in order to break down social barriers between the two communities for future generations. To widen the worldview of the children, one day she brought in a Buddhist monk to give a talk for the children. The monk explained the teachings of Buddhism. The children loved it and ate it up. At the end of the lecture, their hands shot into the air with questions for the Buddhist man.

But humorously, one of the first children Williams called on had an unusual question. In an innocently puzzled voice, he asked, "This is so different; this is amazing! But I still don't understand one thing: are Buddhist monks Catholic or Protestant?"

The children believed that the Catholic-Protestant divide in Ireland shaped the whole world. My first reaction was to laugh when Williams told me the story, but I realized that many of us are no different than those kids. We divide the world into us versus them—those who look like us, have the same cultural background as us, speak our language, and practice the same religion or beliefs, versus those who are different. And many times, we only discover our own prejudices and stereotypes when we're directly faced with them. This is why travel—or inviting others who travel to share their stories—can be a powerful tool for breaking down these assumptions.

Fostering friendships and traveling with those who are different from us is also a great way to challenge stereotypes. In 2015, I was invited by Hands of Peace (a nonprofit that runs projects bringing together Palestinian, Israeli, and American children) to speak at their fundraising event in Chicago. I spoke alongside Elik El-Hanan, an Israeli Jew who is also part of the Bereaved Families Forum.

Elik and I are good friends, and after the event we decided to catch up at a local pub. We called a taxi to pick us up. A few minutes into the ride, the driver asked us where we were from, and I responded that I was from Palestine. He became energetic and proclaimed his support for Palestine but also started repeating a few anti-Semitic tropes: "You are unlucky! If you were occupied by anyone else, you would have been free by now. But the Jews! They control the world," he proclaimed.

I smiled, looked at Elik, and said, "Why don't you tell him where you are from, Elik?" Elik told him that he was an Israeli Jew. The driver, a white American middle-aged man, hit the brakes and looked back at us, mouth agape and eyebrows raised.

"But he's an Arab and you're a Jew! How can you be friends?" the driver exclaimed. He then remembered what he had just said about Jews and tried to justify it. "Look, I am so happy that the Jews are controlling our economy. They are smart and they make sure that things are going well in America." Elik responded, "I am a Jew, and I'm broke. Jews don't control the world."

The two of us decided to tell him our stories. Elik's 14-year-old sister was killed by a Palestinian suicide bomber. Elik was an elite soldier in the Israeli military, but his sister's death led him to conclude that fighting was not the answer. He refused to return to the military for reserve duty and became a peacemaker instead, cofounding an organization composed of Palestinian and Israeli former fighters who had decided to put aside their weapons and fight for peace between Israelis and Palestinians. Elik, his parents, and his two brothers are among my heroes, I told the driver. I don't care about their religion, their ethnicity, or their nationality. My brother was killed by Israeli soldiers, but I don't see Elik as my enemy. Elik's family is my family, and I know he feels the same way about my family.

Because I am Palestinian, my identity seems to prompt an abundance of anti-Jewish sentiments. The moment I mention that I'm Palestinian, some people feel the urge to explain how they don't like Jews and confidently spout conspiracy theories to me. But at the same time, being Palestinian gives me legitimacy that others might not have in countering those narratives and breaking these inaccurate stereotypes. It often shocks people to be told by a Palestinian that, in fact, they shouldn't believe these stereotypes about Jews.

America isn't the only place where I've faced these stereotypes. In 2008, I traveled with Elik's parents (Rami and Nurit) to Egypt, where his father and I were receiving an award for our peace work. It was during the Muslim holy month of Ramadan, when Muslims fast from sunrise to sunset, and I took Rami and Nurit to visit my sister, who lived in a suburb of Cairo. We joined her family for *iftar*—when Muslims break their fast every evening during Ramadan.

After dessert, we took a taxi back to our hotel. My father, who was traveling with us, warned me not to speak Hebrew in the taxi. However, I am used to speaking Hebrew with Rami, so a few minutes into our ride, I forgot my dad's advice and we started speaking Hebrew. The taxi driver looked at me and said, "Is this language that you're speaking what I think it is?" Arabic and Hebrew are both Semitic languages with some similar words, and while the driver didn't speak Hebrew, he knew we were speaking it.

I confirmed his guess: "It is Hebrew," I said. He then decided to lecture me about Israel and the Jews. I listened to him and to all the misinformation he spewed. Once he finished, I answered his questions with respect and quoted him the Quran and the Bible. I also told him Rami and Nurit's story and about their slain daughter. I added that the two of them were advocates for Palestinian human rights.

I ended with a poem by the famous Palestinian poet Mahmoud Darwish in which he says that his first love was with a Jew, and the first judge that sent him to prison was a Jew. He concludes, "I didn't see Jews as devils or angels, but as human beings."

Rami and Nurit were the first Jews this Egyptian had ever met, and he expected them to be anti-Arab, anti-Islam, and combative. They were the opposite of everything he imagined. They were warm and loving, and supported the Palestinian cause of freedom. He'd never heard of Israelis who supported the end of the occupation. This challenged his stereotypes of Jews and complicated his worldview.

Just as we have our own stereotypes, it is almost guaranteed that you will encounter others in your travels who hold prejudices. It's our duty to engage with them with respect and patience, and share stories that can challenge narratives that certain groups are "different," "not civilized," or "dangerous." Every story we share can reach someone's heart.

Travel can be a wonderful form of peace building, because it has the power to change not only stereotypes held by travelers, but stereotypes held by locals. This is why I believe travel is such a powerful tool for opening minds and teaching that the world doesn't have to be based on divisions or hatred. Instead, everywhere we go, we should be finding ways to complicate us-versus-them thinking by highlighting the humanity in everyone. As Darwish concluded in his poem, "I will continue to humanize even the enemy."

I visit Central and South America a few times each year, and they are among my favorite destinations. I have made great friends and quickly become accustomed to the local cultures; I love the food, the music, and nature.

But on my first trip to Brazil, the region and its diverse people were a little-known landscape for me. Many of my friends warned me before my trip, "Brazil is so dangerous." When I went to Mexico for the first time, I heard similar comments: "Why would you go there? Be careful." Yet, Merida, Mexico, ranks 21st among the safest cities in the world, ahead of all United States cities.[1]

I know that my friends want the best for me, and I appreciate their worries. I know that they most likely collected such information from articles with the common headline, "Most Dangerous Cities in Mexico!" Of course, some areas we travel to can be dangerous, and we should consider safety precautions. But when areas are flagged as dangerous, it is important to understand what that means—not all dangers are alike. So how do you balance being safe with being open to new experiences?

First, I've learned from my experiences (and those of my friends) that having common sense while traveling is imperative. For example, my friends in Rio de Janeiro and Buenos Aires told me not to walk on the streets with my iPhone in my hand, because it would make me an easy target for petty theft. My friend Marina's boyfriend, who is Brazilian, had his phone snatched out of his hand at the entrance of a restaurant on a night I was meeting them for dinner.

I also learned to never fight back if someone tries to rob you. When I was in Istanbul, I went to get a drink at Istiklal Street—the main nightlife hub in the city. I entered one of the smaller alleys and walked into a pub, only to find out within a few seconds that I was in a "honeypot" tourist trap. These are venues where a group of ladies will approach and try to drink with you (only to run up a large tab and have their bouncer take you to an ATM, where he robs you), or where a bartender forces tourists to buy a drink for themselves and one of the ladies standing at the bar, only to have her run up a tab. I decided to leave.

I wasn't there for more than a minute, but getting out wasn't as easy as walking in. I was stopped by two aggressive bouncers and punched in the stomach. They screamed that I was refusing to pay an "entrance fee." In this case, standing up to criminals is less important than safety. I handed them $50 and they let me go.

I learned from a friend years ago that it's a good idea to keep a $50 bill on you at all times while traveling because if you are being robbed, they are likely to ignore your other belongings if the amount is worthwhile. I also learned from my friends who got robbed during their travels to never carry all of my credit cards, cash, and forms of identity with me at the same time (and certainly not in the same bag when touring and shopping).

It is helpful to consult the Internet and ask locals, expats, friends, hotels, and guides about common scams and traps. This must be done in a respectful way, not in an accusatory or condescending way. These tips from locals will help you explore your destination without compromising your safety.

I also encourage travelers to review the helpful graphic "40 Tourist Scams to Avoid" at Just the Flight.[2] For instance, the "Flirt" scam makes the list, as does "The Expensive Taxi Driver"—a scam I've encountered countless times in Istanbul, Vietnam, and other destinations. In the taxi scam, the driver will hit the night or traffic surcharge button to run up the meter faster, or claim the meter is broken. Once, for instance, I hailed two taxis for a group in Vietnam, which traveled the same 10-minute distance to the same destination. At the end of the ride, one taxi meter read 160,000 dong ($6.80 USD), and the other meter (which the driver had started with a push of multiple buttons) read 1,070,000 dong ($46 USD). Obviously, I didn't pay $46 for the ride.

I take safety issues seriously. That said, I also don't let every scary article or negative story about a place stop me from visiting. It's sad that some of my friends will write off half the world because they think traveling there is too dangerous. It serves to perpetuate inaccurate stereotypes about these places.

I've met people in Washington, DC, and Baltimore who tell me they are scared to go to a certain country because they think it's violent. But in reality, their home cities have far higher murder and crime rates than those places they are scared of traveling to. St. Louis, Missouri, for instance, ranks as the 15th most dangerous city in the world.[3] I was invited to a major travel conference in St. Louis two years ago, and I didn't hear of anyone refusing to attend the conference because of safety concerns.

The point is, we tend to minimize safety issues in our own country and exaggerate them in other countries that we are less familiar with. It doesn't add up logically, but that's how stereotypes work.

As a result, I encourage people to use common sense and talk to their tour operator or hotel concierge about safety concerns. If you're wandering around certain neighborhoods at night wearing your best fur and pearls, it can be dangerous. Talk to locals and speak with your tour operator about safety concerns. By doing so, we learn how to navigate risks and take the necessary precautions. After all, the dangers are often not much different from those we face at home.

The world has all kinds of people, and as travelers we will encounter racists, bigots, and criminals. But we should not let these people dictate our lives, ruin our travels, or threaten our peace. We should also not engage in fights with those who mistreat us. If there is an opportunity for a conversation, then I will choose to engage. However, shouting matches and reactive negativity almost never change people's views or behavior.

Instead, one of the best ways to deal with fear and prejudice is to be prepared. To this end, there are a few steps I advise people to take:

- Don't let films and media influence your opinion about places you've never visited.

- Be reflective. What assumptions do you have about the destination you are visiting? What assumptions might the people there have about you?

- Use your travels to break down your own stereotypes and the stereotypes that others might have about you.

- Educate by sharing stories (not arguing about politics). Be patient and give people time to process new information.

- Educate yourself about common safety concerns and scams in the destination you are visiting. Ask locals what you should know about safety, and review the helpful graphic "40 Tourist Scams to Avoid This Summer" at Just the Flight.

- Ask your tour operator about any travel warnings that have been issued for your destination and if they are area-specific.

- Check your foreign ministry information about your travel destination. The US State Department offers details on visa requirements, vaccinations, and safety issues. You should take travel alerts with a grain of salt, though.

- Exercise due caution (don't flash valuables, enter rough neighborhoods at night, or wander in unfamiliar and potentially dangerous areas unaccompanied by someone familiar with local customs).

- Don't let safety concerns or fears prevent you from exploring new cultures!

Since prejudices are so deeply rooted in us, it will take a long journey for us to truly overcome them. But I have found that travel is one of the best ways to counter stereotypes. It forces us to face our own prejudices and fears. And every time we encounter someone different from us, we have an opportunity to break down stereotypes.

But to do that, we must always be aware and honest with ourselves about those prejudices. So, next time you travel, be attuned to your thoughts, and try to identify your fears and prejudices when you encounter difference. Don't be afraid to ask yourself the hard questions. There is no shame in fighting negative thoughts. I am very grateful for every experience that has shown me my own prejudices and helped me fight them.

On the good side, for every bad experience I've had with people, I've had 10 positive ones. As a result, we shouldn't let fears or prejudices (our own, or those of others) stop us from engaging with people and exploring other cultures.

CHAPTER 8

DISASTER MANAGEMENT 101: WHEN TRAVEL GOES WRONG

THERE IS ONLY one thing you can be sure of when you travel: things will go wrong at some point. There is no perfect trip where everything goes according to plan. However, things that go wrong can be learning opportunities; they can also lead to some of the most profound and amazing travel experiences. This is when having the outlook of a peacemaker while traveling becomes a necessity. I know how challenging it is to remain calm, resolute, and optimistic in the face of travel problems. However, if we travel with the mind-set of a peacemaker, most problems become opportunities, and even when disaster strikes, we can come out the other side stronger.

In 2008, I was flying to Cairo with my Israeli colleague Rami Elhanan to receive the Eisenhower Medallion from People to People International. It was 2008, and Hosni Mubarak was still president of Egypt. His wife, Suzanne, was supposed to present us the award. My invitation had come from Mrs. Mubarak herself.

They booked me a first-class ticket; I had no reason to think anything would go wrong. I was excited; it was my first time flying in first class. After all, I was an invitee of the first lady of Egypt—one of the most powerful people in the country. I landed in Cairo feeling as proud as a peacock showing off his colorful feathers. I was excited for the ceremony and for the award.

I got off the flight, walked to border control, and handed them my papers: Jordanian and Israeli travel documents. Palestinian Jerusalemites always face issues at airports, even when we only need to transfer to another plane. But this time, with my personal invitation letter from the Egyptian first lady and my first-class tickets, I figured landing in Cairo would be a different experience than what I was used to. I thought I was going to get a VIP welcome.

I was wrong.

When I handed the invitation letter to the Egyptian border control officer, I was told that my name was not showing up anywhere in his system; he said he hadn't received any special instructions regarding my arrival. "But how about the letter?" I asked.

"If this letter was really from the first lady, we would have been notified about your arrival," he said. Not only had I arrived in Cairo without a visa; I was also suspected of forging the signature of the first lady. The situation was not looking good for me. I had expected a royal welcome, and instead I was suspected of a crime and found myself in an Egyptian detention center connected to the airport.

This was possibly the worst turn that a travel experience could take. The cell they placed me in was filthy, small, and overcrowded. Prisoners drank water from the bathroom sink and fought over leftover food from the jailers. I was terrified.

Talking to the other men crammed in the small cell only made me more terrified: some detainees had been there for weeks and months. Everyone in the cell had heartbreaking stories of how they had ended up there. There were three Palestinians from Gaza who had just graduated from a university in Algeria. They were on their way back home to Gaza, which doesn't have ports or airports and can only be accessed through Israel or Egypt. However, when they arrived in Egypt, they found out that the border with Gaza had been closed for political and security reasons. They had no visa to any other country, so they were being detained in the cell until the Gaza border reopened.

Making the situation worse, it was the month of Ramadan, when working hours were shortened and government officials were harder to contact. I had been able to send a few frantic text messages to friends and family seeking help before my phone was taken from me. Now, I had to sit and wait, praying that someone had received my message and could contact the Egyptian government on my behalf.

A few hours after sunset, the guard called my name. When I stood up, he yelled, "Who do you know?" I realized that someone had called on my behalf. He wasn't happy about it. I recounted my story again, but he wasn't interested. A half hour later, an army general showed up, the cell door was opened, and I was free to attend the ceremony.

While in detention, I had felt depressed and angry. I was desperate and powerless to do anything about my situation. I couldn't believe that I was being detained on my way to get an award for my peace work. But afterward, I was grateful for the experience. I became much more interested in human rights issues outside of Israel and Palestine; and this experience eventually led me to work in places like Afghanistan, Colombia, and Syria. I learned to care more about human rights abuses, freedom of expression, and conflict resolution practices all over the world. As a result, in the long run I was able to transform my Egyptian travel disaster into an opportunity for improving the lives of others.

Expecting the Unexpected and the Art of Travel Zen

As a person who travels multiple times a month, I have encountered almost every travel problem there is: lost passports, lost luggage, thefts, long airport delays, scary in-flight aircraft issues, problems at hotels, rental car and taxicab accidents, and getting lost. I even once booked a flight to the wrong city, going to Geneva instead of Zurich.

Most of the time, we can't control things like the weather, airplane mechanical issues, lost luggage, and extra charges we didn't plan on. Hotel reservations get lost or mixed up, and if you've booked a group tour, there's no way to tell if other travelers will be complainers. There are also allergies and health challenges you might face in a foreign country.

What makes travel problems more frustrating is that we're often tired (or hungry) when these things happen. Plus, troubles abroad always seem to cost time and money we feel we don't have, since we've already spent thousands of dollars on the trip itself.

Because travel is stressful, tiring, and unpredictable, every time I head to the airport, I start to feel changes in my body, my demeanor, and my attitude. Lines are long, and security checks are irritating and never fun for a Middle Easterner. There are periodic delays, and on top of all of that, I don't enjoy flying; I still don't feel comfortable in a metal tube in the sky. Therefore, it doesn't take much to push my buttons. It also takes reflection and focus on my part not to become irritated or escalate situations.

But while thinking about travel problems can be intimidating, I've learned that these are the moments that jolt us out of our comfort zone and teach us important lessons. With flight cancellations, we learn patience. When our perfectly planned itinerary falls apart, we learn resilience. When important documents are lost or stolen, we learn crisis management.

Perhaps more important, travel hiccups and disasters teach us to reexamine our values and principles. We are forced to ask ourselves what matters most: our plans or the people traveling with us? The hotel error or the humanity of the person who made the error?

In most cases, how we react to the problem is more important than the problem itself. While it is important to be vocal and express dissatisfaction in a firm and straightforward manner (in person and in online reviews), getting angry and holding a grudge against the airline staff, the hotel receptionist, the car rental company, or the restaurant manager rarely improves your experience or the experience of the people traveling with you.

Once, I was flying out of London on British Airways. I had a laptop bag and a small camera bag with me—equivalent to a normal carry-on bag. But when it came time to board, I was told by the staff that I couldn't take my camera bag with me on the plane, since only one carry-on was allowed. I explained to the boarding staff that it was a $4,000 camera, and I would put it under the seat in front of me.

I had been traveling for two months with the same luggage on more than 10 flights, and I had never had a problem. But rules differ between airlines; my attempt at explaining the situation failed. I found myself arguing, getting angry, raising my voice, and saying unnecessary and hurtful things. They were not being reasonable, but that still was not an excuse for me to lose my temper.

On another trip, I took a different approach. I was traveling with my parents (ages 83 and 78 years old at the time), and we were taking a flight from Tel Aviv to Cairo for my nephew's wedding. We arrived at the airport almost four hours early, knowing that as usual, we would need to go through the extra security as Palestinians. After long pre-airport security checks, we were allowed into the terminal. But when we tried to check in at the counter, the clerk snapped at us, yelling that we shouldn't approach the counter. When I asked when we should come back to check in, he continued shouting at us. He was agitated, angry, and not in a good mood. My initial impulse was to argue back, but I didn't. I just smiled and took my parents to sit down. It wasn't easy to control my emotions, but I knew there would be no use getting angry.

Ten minutes later, he announced over the intercom that passengers could check in. We ended up with a different clerk, who was very nice but also was new at her job and didn't know how to call in wheelchairs for my parents. Ironically, the person who had yelled at us a few minutes earlier stepped in and helped get the wheelchairs.

Overall, becoming angry doesn't resolve conflicts. Raising your voice and being disrespectful are the worst things you can do to advance your cause. In London, I was forced to buy another small bag to use as a carry-on and put my important belongings—laptop, camera, medicine, and papers—in the new bag.

Things would have probably similarly ended in frustration if I had gotten angry at the clerk who mistreated us in Tel Aviv. The clerk might not have helped them get wheelchairs, and my parents would have had to pay the price for my anger (and perhaps even miss their flight). But instead, I chose not to take the clerk's behavior as a personal attack on me, and I gave him the benefit of the doubt that he just had had a bad morning.

It's important for us to recognize what irritates us and focus on harnessing our reaction before responding to others. It is also important to remember that airline and airport staff are human too, and just like us, sometimes they make mistakes and have bad days. But as I've learned from numerous experiences, problems only get worse when we react with anger and intolerance.

Don't Let a Bad Travel Experience Ruin an Entire Country

It's important to remember that our anecdotal experiences don't fully represent a country. At times, I have to remind myself that my bad experience is not reflective of the entire country I'm visiting. My experience in Egypt didn't make me paint the whole country in a negative light. On the contrary, I continue to love Egypt and its people.

When I began writing this book, I asked friends to share some of their best and worst travel stories. There were some terrible stories! My friend Heather told me about her bad experience in Rome. Her hotel room was on the top floor of a building with a broken elevator. She went to a show called *Lil' Kim*, to find out that it was only Lil' Kim's song "Magic Stick" blaring from speakers, over and over again. She was awakened at 4 a.m. by a band practicing outside her hotel window. Later, she lost her passport, and a transit strike made it difficult and expensive to reach the embassy and obtain a temporary passport. Twice someone attempted to pick her pocket, and on the way out of Rome, there was a bomb threat against her flight.

Things went wrong on a daily basis for Heather; therefore, she doesn't remember her time in Rome positively. Her husband is Italian, but although they visit Italy occasionally, she still avoids flying through Rome to this day. But upon hearing her stories, two other friends of mine responded by sharing completely opposite experiences. My friend Elizabeth said she had great memories from her visit to Rome—although she jokingly credited this to a bird pooping on her head at the beginning of the trip (a sign of good luck in Italy!).

Our views of the countries we visit are often shaped by our first experiences in the country. It takes a lot of work to avoid becoming prejudiced toward a place because of a bad experience. But our good experiences are also anecdotal, and we can't negate someone's negative experience because ours was good.

Flying out of Ben Gurion Airport in Israel is always my most dreaded experience. I get "Palestinian VIP" treatment, which involves being escorted into a special line for extra security screening. Each time I pass through the airport, unlike other travelers, I'm interrogated at the entrance to the terminal, at check-in, and at a special security line (which includes a strip search, chemical testing and multiple scans of all my belongings, and sometimes confiscation of electronics or backpacks).

It has gotten slightly better over the years, but Ben Gurion remains the most humiliating airport experience in the world for Palestinians. Even arriving at Ben Gurion Airport from abroad, I'm often taken aside for hours of questioning and security checks that mirrored the ones I endured when departing the country.

One time, after landing in Tel Aviv following a trip to the United States, I was taken into a room by security. I was asked to sit while my luggage was put through an x-ray machine. A few minutes later, about six or seven men dressed in black suits and wearing earpieces rushed into the room.

Before I realized what was happening, the black-clad men picked me up and shoved me against the wall and forced my arms up. They started with a cavity search and demanded that I remain facing the wall. I had no idea what was going on, but I knew I was in deep trouble. I tried to ask what was happening, but the men yelled at me. I was consumed with fear, anger, and powerlessness. There was nothing I could do to change the situation.

Officers were going in and out of the room whispering to each other. I was asked about my boarding pass and where I had sat on the plane. Two minutes later, an airport evacuation alert was put in place. With every new development, I sunk deeper into despair. That was when one of the security officials asked another official, "Does he know?" I turned back and said in frustration, "I don't know anything. What's wrong?" The security official responded that they had found what looked like a bomb in my bag. I was speechless.

My mind started racing. A bomb? I was positive I hadn't packed a bomb! I mean, I would have remembered if I had. My bags were searched in the United States before I boarded the flight. Then I began wondering if someone had planted a bomb in my bag. But who would do that? And why me? I was panicking.

Eventually, a woman in a black suit entered. She went to the x-ray machine monitor, then allowed me to turn around and face her. "Tell me what you have in the smaller bag," she demanded. I listed off all the belongings I could remember. Then she smiled grimly and said, "I think I know where the misunderstanding happened." Immediately my despair was replaced with hope. I might not be spending my life in an Israeli prison after all.

While in the United States, I had purchased a large cowboy-style belt buckle, and at the airport I had bought a bottle of scotch whisky as a gift for a friend. The security official said that next to each other, the two looked like a bomb. I was relieved. This relief lasted for a few hours after they released me (without an apology)—and then I increasingly felt angry and humiliated.

The point is, if I based my relationships with Israelis on my airport experiences, I never would have become a peacemaker. I still believe that my airport experiences in Ben Gurion are unjust and that racial profiling is wrong. But I do not let that stop me from building alliances with Israelis who are trying to change that reality.

Ultimately, we all will face frustrating, infuriating, painful, or even humiliating experiences in our lives. We use these experiences as casus belli for writing off or hating entire groups of people. We can let these experiences govern us—altering our mood, our opinions, and who we are as people. Or, we can reflect on what our experiences have to teach us, using difficult experiences to practice resilience, and using disasters in our lives as a platform for modeling constructive responses and ways to fight for a more just and humane society. Adversity and suffering transform us—but we have the power to decide what that transformation will look like.

It is also important to realize that *who we are* affects how we experience a place. One friend of mine spoke to me about her travels in Africa and the absurd amount of attention she received as a white woman living in Tanzania for two years. At first, the attention was tolerable, but it soon became a daily source of irritation and frustration. It was difficult for her to even go to the shop to buy eggs without having bystanders shout at her on the street with the word "*Mzungu*" ("foreigner" in Swahili) or having random people approach her to ask for money.

But she took away positive lessons from these experiences. She said that in the United States, white people rarely have to be aware of the color of their skin; they don't have to be concerned that someone is treating them or perceiving them in a certain way because they are white. It's quite easy in the United States to carry on your day as a white person without ever being aware of your skin color.

Tanzania forced her to be hyper-aware of her skin color, including the histories, injustices, and privileges that come with it. No one likes to be judged by the color of his or her skin, but in Tanzania she learned that it was important to understand the inequalities and histories that her skin represented. She learned to avoid stepping outside when children were let out of school (as they were often the worst when it came to screaming *"Mzungu!"* at her).

She also learned that this was only one aspect of her life there; she adapted to these realities and went on to meet compelling individuals and make lifelong friendships. Similarly, we must not let bad experiences keep us from engaging with the destinations we visit.

Let Locals Help

During one of my first trips to the United States, almost 20 years ago, I was flying to Los Angeles and had a transfer in New York at LaGuardia Airport. After some questions from border control, I collected my luggage and raced to make it to my next flight. But when I arrived at the security check, I realized that my two travel documents were missing. I frantically checked my pockets and bags, but they were nowhere to be found. And unlike replacing a regular passport, it's a nightmare to get a temporary travel document replaced as a stateless person.

Facing disaster, I decided to do something I always avoided and feared as a Palestinian: I found a police officer and explained the situation. This was an act that filled me with trepidation.

Growing up in Jerusalem, I rarely had positive experiences with police officers (who were almost always Israeli). But here in New York City, I was desperate.

The police officer began calling his colleagues, checking lost and found, and tracing back my steps with me in case I had dropped the documents somewhere. After about 20 minutes, we found my travel documents on a luggage cart, where I had apparently left them after rechecking my bags.

The officer looked at my documents and saw that one of them was from Israel. He asked if I was Israeli. I told him I was Palestinian—and he replied that he was Jewish. For the next few minutes, as he walked me back to the security line—helping me bypass the crowds—we chatted about politics and about Israel and Palestine. We disagreed politically, but it didn't matter; at no point did he treat me differently because of my political opinions. When we separated, we hugged. This was my first positive experience with law enforcement, and I wouldn't have had this experience if I hadn't lost my documents.

Getting Robbed

Chris is a longtime friend of mine. We play soccer together in DC and are both part of the BMW Responsible Leaders' Network. In 2018, Chris was considering moving to Germany to take a position as the CEO of a social enterprise working with refugees. So, he flew to Germany for a job interview.

The morning of the interview (which was scheduled for 1 p.m.), he woke up in his Airbnb and immediately sensed that something was wrong. He walked to the dining room and found that a window was open. He didn't remember opening that window the night before. He looked around and realized that his phone and wallet were missing. Someone had broken into the apartment and stolen his belongings.

Chris still had to go to his job interview with no phone, no cash, and no credit cards. Fortunately, the thief hadn't stolen Chris's laptop. He wrote a post on Facebook about what had happened and told those trying to reach him to be patient with his slow responses. Soon after, a friend living in Germany stepped in and offered to give him a few hundred Euros.

He still had to get to the job interview and navigate the rest of his trip, however, with no phone or map to find his way. To do so, he relied on the generosity of everyday Germans. Each day he was there, instead of taking taxis and Uber, he walked and took public transportation, asking for directions when he lost his way. And ultimately, the interview went well and he was invited to the final interview. As Chris told me of asking help from Germans, "I never would have had this amazing experience if I hadn't gotten robbed and lost my phone and wallet."

Many people worry about getting robbed while traveling. Some travelers will go to Europe but not to South America or Africa out of fear of crime. But you can get robbed anywhere, and if it does happen, it's not the end of the world. Technology has made it much easier to have money sent from anywhere.

Obviously, we should always take safety precautions: spread out documents and valuables among bags; have photocopies or pictures of passports; keep money and credit cards in zippered interior pockets of bags, coats, and purses; and be attentive in crowded places (especially high-risk places like busy tourist sites). But if the worst happens and you get robbed, don't let such an experience beat you down or destroy the rest of your trip.

Stop, Breathe, Reflect, Act

The more I travel, the more I'm grateful for the difficult moments in my travel experiences, because they've taught me invaluable lessons. These moments have forced me to rely on others and often enhanced my appreciation of the places I've visited.

When traveling, something is always bound to go wrong. It can be small, like a couple of hours' delay, or more problematic, like landing in jail or discovering that you don't have a hotel reservation. We also can face emotional challenges, like finding ourselves being mistreated or profiled.

These challenges are not pleasant, and they can ruin trips. But they don't have to. We can decide to respond with patience, courtesy, and kindness instead. We cannot control the weather, the airline schedule, the hotel manager's attitude, or the taxi driver's decision to overcharge us, but we can control how we respond in each of these situations. And a few tips can help us manage even the most difficult situations:

- Expect the unexpected when traveling. Do not demand that things run perfectly, and be flexible when your schedule gets derailed.

- Stop, breathe, and reflect before responding to a roadblock. First, focus on your bodily state (Am I hungry? Tired? Tense? Nervous? Afraid? Worried about money?). Second, consider what response is best for you and those around you. Then and only then, move your focus to the problem.

- Be relentlessly positive. It's good for your health, and it's good for those traveling with you.

- Try to think of disaster as a challenge, a learning opportunity, or a moment to model humanity.

- Let locals (and other travelers) help. You don't have to face trouble alone, and you might be surprised by the kindness of strangers.

In short, when we travel, we surrender a lot of our control. But there is one thing we don't surrender: regardless of where we go, we always have the power to respond positively when things go wrong. We have the power to be angry or to be peaceful. We can feel attacked or frustrated or yell; or we can choose to be thoughtful, kind, and respectful.

So, the next time you face a roadblock, instead of focusing on what is going wrong for you, try to focus on being good to others. Help someone who is lost, pay the grocery or restaurant bill for a stranger, ask people if they need assistance, leave generous tips, and give well-thought compliments. Because acts of kindness are powerful, and they can help transform bad experiences into good ones.

CHAPTER 9

A WOMAN'S PERSPECTIVE

By Ellie Cleary

ELLIE IS A TRAVELER and tourism professional who believes that true connection comes through cups of tea with strangers and pushing ourselves to do what scares us. You can follow her travels on SoulTravel Blog.com.

• • •

FOREWORD: When I started writing this book, I wanted to share my travel stories, challenges I have encountered in the travel industry, and opportunities for transforming tourism. But when I started writing the "How to Meet People While Traveling" chapter, I found myself wondering if my experiences were really all-encompassing. What about women travelers? Did they have the same perspective as I do about traveling alone, getting lost in a city on purpose, and accepting invitations from strangers to visit their homes for a meal?

I started talking to some of my female friends to learn about their perspectives for inclusion in the book. But the more I talked to women, the more I realized that I would not be able to truly represent their perspective. If I were to write a chapter about women traveling, it would lack authenticity and accuracy. Regardless of how much I can empathize, I will never be able to fully understand what women experience while traveling alone.

As a result, I reached out to my friend Ellie Cleary, a blogger who is passionate about solo female traveling. I met Ellie during a travel conference in Amsterdam in summer 2017. Once an executive for a major travel company, she decided to change her focus to travel writing and social activism. Since then, Ellie has been an ally for my work with MEJDI, for which I am extremely grateful.

Ellie has traveled solo around the world. She has told me about the challenges she faces as a solo female traveler, and how she wants to help other female travelers be able to travel solo and not feel they are restricted. As a result, I appreciate her contributing her voice here. Understanding that not everyone has the same travel privileges and experiences (whether due to gender, race, nationality, class, language, or sexual orientation) is an important part of the discussion on socially responsible travel—and I believe that discussing these challenges openly and listening to these voices is an important step in reforming the travel industry and learning how to travel responsibly.

—*Aziz Abu Sarah*

The Hardest Part of the Journey

If it's a dangerous business walking out of our front door, then nowhere is that more true than inside our heads. The scariest part of my journeys, ever since I started travelling—whether for one day or one year—has always been the buildup to leaving.

As women travellers, especially, the world around us is full of reasons not to leave our comfort zones. Friends, family, and loved ones tell us that journeys might not be safe or a good idea; the media are filled with bad news; and no sooner have we decided to travel somewhere than our own minds start to convince us that we've made the wrong decision. You might say that the odds are stacked against us.

Our vision of the world from our homes is always filtered and limited. From comfort zones, it's easy to make judgments and remain in our regular modus operandi, which is why it's vital to get out there and explore.

Travelling in a way that lays us open is perhaps the ultimate act of surrender, and admission, that not everything is as we read it in the paper or are told it on the news. Solo journeys are those that push us—with finding our own resourcefulness and inner strength when things go wrong.

At no time has this been more true for me than before setting off on my trip to Iran in 2017.

At the start of each year, I like to make a note of the places I'd most like to experience in the upcoming year. It's usually a mix of places near and far from home, places to go back to as well as new countries, and that year Iran made it to the top of my list. Intrigued by what I'd read about Iran, I decided that I wanted to see Iran for myself, despite the complexities of travelling there on a British passport. I booked my flights and started making plans.

As soon as I announced my plans to travel there, my family and friends did their best to convince me what a bad idea it was. From my mother's fears of my ending up in an Iranian jail accused of spying to friends remarking, "I hope you're not becoming an extremist," when the time came to board the plane, I was very nervous.

On the flight from Istanbul, my Iranian experience began. Seeing me alone on the plane, one Iranian couple promptly said hello, asked me about my travels, and requested if their daughter could sit next to me to practice her English (the daughter seemed less enthusiastic about this idea). I got a full insight into life in

Tehran—the best places to eat, how to wear my headscarf and look stylish, and the best night markets—before even landing.

I'd had a similar experience getting my Iranian visa. As I stood in a long line that was filled predominantly with dual Iranian-British citizens, two women quickly started a conversation with me. An hour later, I had more than a handful of invitations for dinner for when I arrived in Iran and more travel tips than I could handle.

What followed during my time in Iran was nothing less than eye-opening. On my arrival in Tehran, the phone rang in my hotel. It was Mina, my young, female tour guide. I was shocked. I had expected a trip filled with contact with men, as is the norm when travelling in many traditional countries where there is not equal footing between men and women. How could it be that here in Iran—a country that we are taught to believe so many negative things about—I was to be guided by a woman for two weeks when I had found it very difficult to connect with women in more "developed" countries?

Mina was in her early 30s, well educated, and from Shiraz, in the south of Iran. She'd been leading tours around Iran for different operators for the past few years, was a tourism graduate, and spoke flawless English. And she was somewhat typical of Iranian women: very well educated, women have made up 80 percent of engineering and medical graduates in Iran over recent years and are every bit as feisty as your average New Yorker. I was forced to quickly abandon any ideas I might have had about repression of women in Iran—which is different from what we are led to believe—and to reevaluate all of my assumptions about living and travelling there.

In travel—especially solo female travel—there will always be more people who try to persuade you against your travel ideas than who support them. Even without the advice of others or the media, or (perhaps worst of all) the politically motivated government travel advisories, there have been several other moments when I thought myself to be crazy. The fear about what *could* happen can be crippling.

I'm not the only one who finds stepping out the door (and comfort zone) the hardest part of travel. To the question in a solo female travel Facebook group, "What advice would you give to a woman who wants to solo travel?" the response was overwhelming. Among the dramatic outliers of "Take pepper spray" or "Carry a personal alarm," the majority response was this: "Just do it."

The Rise of Solo Female Travel

More women than ever are finding the courage to step out of their doorways, more so than their male counterparts. In a 2014 survey, it was found that 72 percent of the American women asked like to travel alone; while in the UK, 55 percent of respondents to another solo travel survey were female.[1]

Ever since the invention of the bicycle—which allowed women to get around independently for the first time in modern history—the female travel movement has been growing. In recent decades, solo travel has taken on new meaning. Solo travel is no longer regarded as a luxury or frivolous experience of simply seeing new sights or an exotic getaway, but rather as a journey of transformation.

Despite all of its clichés and the ensuing waves of tourists going to Bali in search of "healing," there's a reason why *Eat Pray Love* has sold more than 12 million copies. We understand that taking a journey alone offers entirely different opportunities than, say, a family vacation or a trip with friends.

It also means that, increasingly, women—regardless of their relationship status or age—embark on solo trips around the world. Solo female travel is a choice for many women who have plenty of alternative travel partners. Why? Because solo travel is different. I know that the majority of my most transformative travel experiences were when I was alone. It's not that there's anything wrong than travelling with friends, partners, and family, but the experience as a solo traveller is different. We are forced to open our eyes and be more in tune with our surroundings; and, perhaps most of all, as a solo traveller we are more open to connect: with new natural surroundings, with new cultures, and with new friends.

As our demand for deeper and more transformative experiences grows, we are becoming aware that often the ideal way to access these is through solo travel.[2]

Open vs. Closed: Staying Safe When We Travel

There's a reason why setting off on a trip is so often the hardest part: We imagine all of the things that *could go wrong*. From getting stranded to being harassed to feeling overwhelmed by a new place, the list of things that could happen is long.

But once we set off, the reality is often different. Sometimes the fears all melt away; sometimes we learn how to deal with them better. Sometimes we are tested. For me, the question I've often asked myself is this: How can I travel and remain open to the experiences and people that I meet, acting from an open-hearted place as opposed to closing myself down, constantly on the lookout for any perceived risk?

Wandering the streets of Yogyakarta, Indonesia, I was in search of the entrance to the famous Sultan's Kraton (Palace). I'd been busy reading about it in my guidebook and heeded the warnings about people loitering outside, trying to direct travellers to a "fake version" of the Kraton (essentially a scam involving paying a higher entrance fee to enter only a small museum about the Kraton rather than the Kraton itself). Armed with my insider knowledge, I set off in search of the entrance.

In the days before local SIM cards were readily available, I had only my book's map to find my way. Walking the perimeter, I quickly came across a group of local men, who asked me if I was looking for the Kraton entrance. Congratulating myself for being clued in on the scam, I determinedly ignored them. What followed was my walking the perimeter twice in search of the entrance, without luck. Eventually I was forced to go back to the same spot, to find out that all along they were correct: the entrance was right there, and they had been trying to help a lost tourist. No ulterior motives.

The joke was on me.

If we do our research before we travel (which we should), chances are we'll know what to watch out for. But what if we also learn to become suspicious of strangers?

Of course, there are cases when it goes the other way.

Some of my most testing experiences have been on my solo trips in India. Midway through my solo travels around Rajasthan, it was time to move on from Jodhpur, the beautiful blue city, to Jaisalmer, by train. Clambering into the three-tiered sleeper AC carriage, I was surprised to find I'd been assigned the lower berth, as opposed to the upper berth of the three, which I usually go for. (Why? As a woman, you're out of reach and subject to fewer prying eyes if you're up two tiers than on the bottom berth.) Above me was a Chinese solo female traveller; opposite me was a tall Indian man, who—I'd later find out—was in the army. Tired from getting on the train at midnight, I quickly fell asleep.

I awoke at about 3 a.m. to strange noises and the feeling that something was wrong. Sitting bolt upright on my bunk and pulling off my eye mask, I found the man opposite me sitting on the edge of his bunk, eyes glued to me, masturbating.

Shouting at him, I ran off to find the carriage attendant, who was nowhere to be found.

Returning to my berth, I found the man now hiding under his sheet and the girl above me awake and asking me what had happened. I spent the rest of the night sleepless on a spare upper berth at the other end of the carriage. At about 6 a.m., the train attendant reemerged, and I reported the situation to him. He brought in the man in question to apologise to me, and what followed was probably one of the most awkward moments of my life. I could not look him in the eye, nor could I accept his apology. I also did not want to take the matter further. If I reported him, he would lose his army career.

I've never been so relieved to get off a train.

In the days that followed in Jaisalmer, I felt a deep distrust. Where I had previously been open and willing to think the best, I was now fearful of any man I came across. My mind kept asking me, was I dreaming, did I make the whole thing up? Most of all, I was angry that the incident had spoiled my love of train travel. I had to get away from Jaisalmer and the heavy feeling in my stomach. But the predatory energy was far from gone. My guesthouse owner in Jaisalmer was creepy at best.

Figuring that there was no time like the present to get over my fears and (literally) get back on the train, I booked a train to go to Delhi the next day.

But it was not meant to be.

I arrived at the Jaisalmer station around midnight (many trains leave in the middle of the night in India), only to hear announcements that my train was running 10 hours late—which meant it would be arriving at 11 the following morning. It was too late to get in a rickshaw alone, and no hotels were answering their phones. After I spoke to the station manager, it became clear that there was only one thing to do: sleep in the station.

Fortunately, this is not an uncommon thing in India, where trains can run days late. I sat down among the groups of people in the waiting rooms; sleep did not come. When it got light at around 7 a.m., I officially aborted the mission and went to a hotel, only to find out later that it was owned by a man who had reportedly harassed other female travellers.

I canceled my ticket to Delhi and instead got on a train to Bikaner in northern Rajasthan the following night, to connect onward from there instead.

Turns out, my original train to Delhi never did show up.

The purpose of this story is not to scare anyone off travelling to India. My good stories about India far outnumber the bad ones. But there are a few learnings I took from the experience.

Jaisalmer felt bad to me. Whether it was because of my train experience or because of the energy of the place, I don't know. It just felt bad. If you find yourself in a place that doesn't feel good, leave. We have a choice and a responsibility for what situations we allow ourselves to remain in, after all.

Confidence and standing up for yourself is a necessary part of life and solo travel. Walking with your head held high, knowing a few basic self-defense moves, and most of all trusting your own judgment and intuition are invaluable.

On many of my solo trips, I've had to fake confidence. In South Asian countries in particular, the best thing to do if a man tries something out of line is to shout at him and shame him in public. You'll likely find all of your neighbors coming to your defense. But as I'm a Brit who was taught to be reserved and not show emotions, this does not come naturally to me. I've had to push myself.

I never advocate travelling with pepper spray, but I do advocate finding something that will help you feel tough and confident in case you need it. For some, that's taking a self-defence course. For others, it might be a necklace or piece of jewellery that reminds you of your strength. For me, it's finding my inner strength that I know I can draw on when I need it. Find what resonates with you.

The Rajasthan story continued, and took another turn.

From Bikaner (which I had left Jaisalmer to go to), I joined a train for the 17-hour journey to Haridwar in Uttarakhand. Boarding my train, I was immediately greeted by a friendly family sharing the same cluster of berths. Silently, I breathed a massive sigh of relief. As I chatted away with their daughter for half the trip, this family shared their food with me, and they even went and found the right bus to Rishikesh for me when we reached Haridwar. Children from the next set of berths kept stopping by to show card tricks, proudly giggling and practicing their English all the way.

This was the Indian train journey experience that travellers speak of and write about. To this day, the family has no idea how deeply grateful I am for their warmth on that journey, even though I am still in touch with their daughter.

It's good to bear in mind that many countries that are portrayed as dangerous in travel advisories and media are not necessarily more dangerous than the countries we leave behind to travel. Sometimes it's the opposite. Statistically, more sexual assaults happen every year with visitors to Spain, the United States, France, Thailand, and many other countries than they do in India. But the Indian ones get all the press coverage.[3]

My favourite line of most UK government travel advisories is this: "Over 940,000 British nationals visited India in 2017. Most visits are trouble-free."[4] I think it's this mentality we have to travel with. I believe that 95 percent of the people we meet on our travels will be good. They are people who are looking to welcome us or help us, or are simply curious—particularly in the less-visited destinations. That number can be 80 or 99 percent—whatever resonates with you. But the point is this: more people out there are well-meaning than are out to get us.

It's up to us to take responsibility for our own safety as much as we can and establish our own rules and boundaries to keep us secure when we travel. For some people, that means wearing a wedding ring and saying you're married (regardless of the truth). For others, it means never sharing your travel plans with strangers. We also learn along the way from our mistakes, experiences, and advice from others.

I learned the hard way about social media sharing. I prefer not to share social media photos, videos, or stories while I'm still in a place, especially if it's related to where I'm staying or gives my specific location away. Once a friend tagged me in a public Facebook post about the guesthouse we were staying in. A would-be Romeo who saw the post showed up the next day (only to be reported to the police, who acted swiftly).

There are a few essential tips for female travellers that I'd recommend following or at least thinking about, especially when travelling to countries that are more conservative than your own:

- Always let someone at home or a trusted friend know where you are, especially if you're on your own or going somewhere remote.

- Don't share with strangers your travel plans, the fact that you're travelling alone, or where you are staying.

- Research your destination before going there—learn about the cultural norms if they are different from your own.

- Take your cues from local women. If you're not sure whether it's safe to go somewhere at night, check to see if there are other women out alone. If not, stay in your hotel or ask hotel staff for advice.

- Take your guidance on how to dress from other women too. If all local women of your age are covering their legs and shoulders, it is probably not the best idea to go out in shorts and a tank top.

- Get a local SIM card if you can. Being able to access Google Maps in an emergency helps prevent scams (taxi detours, shopping tours?) and can be reassuring in case you need it.

- If you are invited to tea with men whom you are happy to chat with, then agree to meet in public—especially in countries where it may not be normal for men to interact freely with women they are not related to. Make sure that people know where you are. There's a big difference between meeting a single man and meeting a family.
  If you're invited to dinner with a family, if the invitation comes from a woman, take that as a good sign. If it's just a man, you should do a little digging to see if women will be around too.

- Apply distancing strategies with men who you may feel have ulterior motives. In Asian countries, calling a man "brother" or "uncle" (if he's older) sends a clear message.

- Never underestimate the usefulness of dark sunglasses (for avoiding eye contact), a book (for the same), and headphones (if all else fails, to drown out any annoying people trying to talk to you!).

- Don't answer or make up the answer to any personal questions you don't feel comfortable answering.

In some cases, it's tricky to have hard-and-fast rules—you have to trust your judgment. The longer you spend in a country and talk to people, the better idea you'll have about what is good behavior and what to steer clear of.

Just as the vulnerability of solo travel can be a challenge, in some cases it's the reverse.

Travelling back to Dhaka after my time in the Sundarbans, Bangladesh (the world's largest mangrove forest), I felt exhausted. It had been a long day of travel by many different modes of transport, and so I was grateful to be able to relax at an upscale hotel. As I walked into my hotel, it felt as if I were being welcomed as family immediately.

Over drinks on the rooftop terrace with some of the hotel's management team, I mentioned that I'd been thinking of visiting Srimangal and Sylhet (the country's tea region) by train in the next few days. I woke up the next morning to find not only that my train tickets had been booked for me, but also that the hotel was sending along with me one of their receptionists, whose native home and family were in Srimangal. Being used to solo travel and making my own travel plans, and also just a little bit stubborn, I protested. I said that it was too much, that I'd be just fine on my own. But my objections fell on deaf ears.

And so I explored Srimangal and Sylhet in the company of kind and fun Jubayer, who had worked before as a tour guide for the region of Srimangal and was now working at the Dhaka hotel, sent along as my chaperone. Over the days, a pattern emerged: meeting his family and friends, and receiving countless invitations to lunch and dinner by strangers we met along the way as we travelled around. I saw some of the most beautiful tea gardens and parts of Sylhet district, thanks to his knowledge. We shared jokes over endless coconut waters and photo opportunities, and I came to understand a little more about Bangladeshi culture.

Having Jubayer show me around as a local was the ultimate luxury and also just one example of the kindness that I experienced in Bangladesh.

But it also showed how difficult solo female travel can be in some places. As persistent as some of the stares and friendly hellos that a solo (foreign) female traveller gets in Bangladesh are the strategies to protect her.

Protect her from what? you may wonder. In my case, clearly the people I met felt a responsibility to look after me, which included making sure I did not travel alone.

While I was in Bangladesh, I spoke to some strong, independent-minded ladies who had travelled solo; notably, they had travelled solo to places in Southeast Asia and Europe, but *they had not travelled solo in Bangladesh*. Why? To a large extent, it seemed to be because solo female travel is just not accepted as a concept in Bangladesh. People tend to assume that a woman travelling alone is a problem—she needs protecting or is inviting the wrong kind of company.

Opportunities for women in Bangladesh to discover their own country, alone, are pretty much nonexistent.

The Triple Standard

While solo female travel is growing in popularity today, the vast majority of resources, content, and even voices out there tell of solo female travel from a Western, white perspective (including me). The voices and resources available for female travellers outside of North America and Europe, and particularly for women from patriarchal cultures, are severely lacking.

Solo female travellers are still majority white, well-educated women from privileged backgrounds. While there are increasing numbers of travellers from other ethnicities, they are still underrepresented. This is important, because our experiences are different. Somewhere that it would be easy for a white woman to explore might provide a very different experience for a woman of colour. In some cultures, white skin is prized and valued, and dark skin is looked down on. In many parts of the world, far too often, how we are received depends on the perceived value of our passport and the shade of our skin.

When women from traditional societies (where they have less freedom) travel, they often travel outside of their own countries, because they are not free to explore their own. As I sat next to an Indian girl at Muscat Airport waiting for a flight to Chennai, she asked me, "Why are you travelling to India alone?" Our conversation revealed that she loved travelling by herself too, but she'd "never do it in India." I've seen the same in other countries.

Part of it comes from wanting to go out and see the world, but undoubtedly part of it comes from the attitudes toward solo female travellers in those countries. As many a friendly "uncle" has told me, "It is not advisable for women to travel alone."

This needs to change. Travel should be a right, but in so many cases it is still a privilege. The opportunity is not equal. Let's do what we can to fix that.

Crossing the Border

In the current (literal) climate, many point out the impact of travelling and its less-than-positive carbon footprint. But even in the age of overtourism and spiraling carbon emissions, we desperately need more of the type of travel that brings more connection.

In summer 2017, 70 years after India and Pakistan's independence from British colonial rule and from their partition from each other, I ended up—unintentionally, and perhaps driven by postcolonial guilt—following the line of the India-Pakistan border. In the kind of exploration that only ever makes sense in hindsight, one of the most poignant moments for me was attending the closing ceremony at the Attari-Wagah border, just a few miles outside of Amritsar.

Every day, as the sun goes down, a spectacle of nationalism and pomp celebrates the closing of the only internationally open border between India and Pakistan. Marching, high kicks, salutes, taunting, and a blink-and-you-might-miss-it handshake are some of the few semblances of diplomacy between these two countries at the moment.

Crowds come to celebrate their might over the other side, and both sides have built huge stadiums that lend the atmosphere of being at a cricket match or other sporting event. But despite the fact that Indians and Pakistanis sit within 20 meters of each other, the middle is fiercely guarded and obscured from the other side by strategically planted trees. That the people sitting on either side of this line both speak Punjabi, dress the same, and eat the same food is deliberately obscured.

After all, it's much easier to make an enemy of people who don't look exactly the same as you.

There's a darker side to the Wagah ceremony in the nationalism it stirs, but if even one of the hundreds of visitors realises that not all is as we are told by politically driven media, it's worth it.

And this is why we need to cross the border: to realise that the "other" is just the same as we are.

CHAPTER 10

FOSTERING INTERRELIGIOUS EXCHANGE THROUGH TRAVEL

MY FATHER AND mother came to visit me in Washington, DC, for the first time in November 2018. He was 82 years old at the time and didn't speak English, but that didn't stop him from trying to talk to random strangers at the mall, the park, and elsewhere.

It was hard to find activities for my parents to do during their stay, since they couldn't walk long distances, and their lack of English hindered them from exploring on their own. However, my father unexpectedly fell in love with mini golf on his trip. After five minutes, he became a professional. He was skilled enough that he asked the staff at the mini golf course if there was a US mini golf competition he could sign up for.

But nothing could prepare me for the surprise that my father threw at me next. When Friday came, he wanted to go pray at a mosque. I called my friend Fadwa, whose uncle went to pray at the mosque every Friday. She suggested that I send my dad with her uncle so they could visit the mosque together.

I drove my father to Fadwa's uncle's house, where they were waiting for us. My dad and Fadwa's uncle hit it off immediately and sauntered off to the mosque together.

On our way home, I asked my father about his mosque visit and his conversations with Fadwa's uncle. He said it was great to learn how Muslims live in the United States. I then asked, "How was the mosque—did you like it?" He told me they had tried to go to the mosque, but it was full.

"So what did you do? Pray outside?" I asked, curious. In Jerusalem, when you go to a mosque and it's full, you normally pray outside. But I was worried because it was the end of November and the temperature was very cold. "I'm sorry," I added, "I'm sure it was cold outside."

My father shot me a mischievous glance. "No," he said. "We prayed at a synagogue." I turned to him, a bit stunned.

"America is crazy," he continued. "Muslims actually pray in synagogues here!" As it turned out, the mosque and synagogue were located next to one another—and when the mosque became too full, the synagogue would open its doors for the Muslims to pray there.

This was a man who had spent most of his life with Jews all around him in Jerusalem, but he had never set foot in a synagogue. His first time doing so was in the United States; and he didn't just visit a synagogue, he prayed inside one. This was one of the last things he would have expected to do in the United States. I asked him what he thought of the synagogue. He said, "It was great!"

The experience was so impactful for him that when we got home, the first thing he did was start calling friends and family back home in Jerusalem. He would start off trying to contain his excitement. "Yeah, America is nice. I miss being in Jerusalem." But then he would quickly exclaim, "Guess where I prayed?"

Our friends and family would respond, "We assume you prayed in a mosque."

"Nope!" my father would reply enthusiastically. "In a synagogue!" Our family members and friends were surprised and confused by this answer. "Did they convert you to Judaism?" one of them asked, teasingly. Another asked, "What has Aziz done to you?" My father responded, "No, in America the Muslims rent the synagogue for space and then they go and pray there!"

I have many Muslim friends who have never been to a house of worship that was not a mosque. This is not unique to Muslims: most people around the world have never been to someone else's house of worship.

While my father's visit wasn't during a Jewish service, it was still meaningful; he was able to attend a religious service in another group's house of worship—and that on its own was powerful enough to help him see "the other" a bit differently.

Be Curious

I grew up in a conservative Muslim family, going to the mosque each Friday. Etched deep into my memory is the sound of the call to prayer echoing through the neighborhood, accompanying my father to the mosque, and greeting people for prayers.

These memories are woven together in the complex embroidery that connects me to my family, my tribe, my city, and my culture. There were no churches or synagogues in my neighborhood, and no Christians in my school; our primary school was all Sunni Muslim. Still, I would discuss with my Muslim friends the differences in our religious cultures: we thought we knew everything about Christianity, when in reality we knew nothing.

My friends and I did express some curiosity about what church was like. What did it look like from the inside and the outside? What was the difference between a mosque and a church? One day, we decided to go see for ourselves.

We walked through Damascus Gate and wound our way through the narrow cobblestoned alleys of the Old City, headed toward Jerusalem's most famous church: the Church of the Holy Sepulchre. This was believed to be the site of Jesus's Crucifixion, burial, and Resurrection.

We struggled to find our way to the church: we didn't have Google Maps in those days, and although we were from Jerusalem, we had never been in the alleys of the Christian Quarter. This area of the Old City was a mysterious place to us.

We eventually stumbled upon the Holy Sepulchre and cautiously walked up to admire its complex and beautiful exterior. We were told in school that a Muslim family holds the keys to the gates of the Holy Sepulchre and has held on to those keys for almost 1,000 years. Depending on whom you speak to, there are various stories behind why a Muslim family would hold the keys to one of the holiest Christian sites.

Some see it as a symbol of tolerance and the unique relationship between Muslim and Christians in the Holy Land. Others see it as a form of control, representing a Muslim takeover of the city. And still others believe it's because the denominations sharing the church couldn't decide among themselves which should keep the keys.

We walked into the church, afraid but curious. We didn't know how we should act in a church. Was it like a mosque? Should we take off our shoes? We looked around and noticed that the churchgoers still had their shoes on inside. We thought that was bizarre. For us, if you enter a holy site, you must take off your shoes to not dirty the space.

We walked in with our shoes still on but didn't think about our hats. As soon as we stepped in, a religious man dressed in black with a large cross on a chain hanging all the way down to his belly—we didn't know what a priest was at that time—walked up to us and did not look happy.

"He knows we're Muslim," we all said to each other at the same time. We were not supposed to be there, and we had been exposed. But instead, the man ordered us to take off our hats. We complied, relieved that we had made it through the entrance without raising too much suspicion.

Inside, we found scores of worshippers touching and kissing a large rock on the ground. There were large, intimidating murals and flickering candles. It was very different from what we were used to at our mosques. But there were also aspects that were similar. I've seen people enter the Dome of the Rock—located in the Al-Aqsa Mosque compound—and touch the site where the Prophet Muhammad is believed to have ascended into heaven. In the church, I saw Christians doing the same thing—lining up to touch the surface of the stone, believed to be the rock on which Jesus was anointed for burial.

We walked around the church, in awe of the paintings, architecture, and rituals. However, despite taking the first step in visiting a church for the first time, I felt that something about the experience was still lacking. I wasn't able to fully understand what it was like to be Christian, or how Christians connected to God. I saw Christians and learned a few things, but our whole visit lasted just a few minutes. We visited a few more times after that, but we never stayed long enough to understand how Christians practiced their faith or rituals.

It was just several years later when I attended church with an American girl in Jerusalem that I began to experience more of the Christian faith. I only went because I thought this cute blond woman was inviting me on a date; with my limited English at the time, I thought she had invited me to a concert (she had mimed something about singing). But instead, she had invited me to come hear her sing in the church choir!

I walked down the aisle of the Jerusalem YMCA (a common venue for both church services and concerts) and searched the room for her. Suddenly, however, the service started, and everyone began singing in Arabic and English a song: "I Have Decided to Follow Jesus."

The minister confirmed my fears, as he welcomed everyone to the church. I thought to myself, "This must be a mistake. I'm not supposed to be here." But I was too embarrassed to leave, so I stayed for the entire service. This was the first time I had truly taken part in a Christian ritual—and it was an unbelievable experience. I loved the music and the sermon, which was titled "Love Your Enemies."

Suspend Judgment

Since that day, whenever I travel, I try to learn more about other faiths and even attend religious services when appropriate. I've joined Buddhist, Jewish, Christian, and Hindu services. Most of the time, I don't understand the language (in Ireland, for instance, people were praying in Gaelic). But there's something very special and humbling about experiencing other people's rituals and understanding their faith.

So how do we approach other religious faiths in a way that is appropriate and respectful? A few easy steps we can take are to be curious, suspend judgment, and set aside what we think we know about the group we're visiting. Curiosity is important, but if we approach a community thinking we know everything about them (the way I approached the Christian church I visited), we're far less likely to walk away having learned anything.

Suspending judgment is especially important, since we all grow up with entrenched ideas about who "they" are and what "they" believe. I grew up as a Sunni Muslim (almost all Palestinian Muslims are Sunni). Our educational system taught us nothing good about other Muslim sects. I still remember watching news coverage of the Iran-Iraq war on television as a boy, and rooting for the Iraqis because they were real (Sunni) Muslims, while the (Shia) Iranians were infidels.

When I started traveling, I decided to visit a Shia mosque for the first time. In the back of my mind, I still believed they weren't real Muslims. But to my surprise, the Shia mosque was very similar to a Sunni mosque. The differences were so small, and the similarities between Sunnis and Shias were greater than I had ever imagined. I realized that the anti-Shia propaganda I was fed growing up had nothing to do with facts. (Today, my Shia friends tell me they grew up hearing similar anti-Sunni propaganda.)

In the summer of 2019, I also had the chance to experience a completely different kind of Muslim ritual: a Sufi dhikr. I was visiting Sarajevo in Bosnia and Herzegovina. My friend Ziyah contacted a local Sufi order and asked if our group of Americans could attend a service. In the ritual, Sufi Muslims chant about God using verses from the Quran, punctuated by heavy breathing and back-and-forth swaying and bowing movements. I grew up in a Muslim family, but I had never seen anything like this. It was educational, moving, and spiritual.

Overall, if we approach other religious communities with the same spirit of humility, respect, and learning that we extend to others, we'll discover both a world of diversity and surprising similarities. But we have to be willing to suspend judgment and approach the existence of others with different beliefs as a learning opportunity, not as a threat.

Have a Q&A with a Devotee

When I went to Vietnam in 2016, I visited many Buddhist and Confucian temples. I was transfixed by the carved wooden interiors, the gold-decorated lacquered-wood statues, and the devotees lighting incense and folding their hands in prayer before the altars. But after visiting almost a dozen temples, I began to feel something was missing.

I never understood the varying religious views in Vietnam or how the people practice these beliefs. I tried reading about it, but the meaning of the strange rituals still made no sense to me. Buddhism is different than the Abrahamic faiths, which I am much more accustomed to. I learned very quickly that I can't use the Abrahamic faiths as a reference point for learning about the practices of Eastern religions.

When I returned to Vietnam, I decided to try to understand more about the way the Vietnamese practice their faith. So, I contacted a friend of mine and asked if she knew a Buddhist monk who would be willing to host me and a few friends at a temple. I explained that we were not interested in a temple where tourists congregated but a neighborhood temple where locals went to pray.

My Vietnamese friend found us a temple off the beaten path, on a dirt road in the middle of a cluster of houses. When we walked into the temple, a Vietnamese woman with a shaved head, dressed in a long robe, came out to greet us, and from that moment until the time we left, she never stopped smiling.

She was excited that we wanted to visit her temple and were interested in hearing her story. She sat down with us and began offering us water, juice, and fruit. The entire time we were with her, she constantly asked us, "Is there anything you guys need? Can I get you anything?" Even though I had come expecting a lot of differences between our cultures, I thought that this culture was actually quite similar to Palestinian culture. They will do everything possible to be hospitable and honor their guests.

The temple was a space for female monastics, and we spent several hours learning about the temple, seeing how the monastics practiced their faith, and meeting young people studying to become monks. We heard the woman's story and how she had decided to become a monk. She said that when she was a teenager, she realized that she wasn't interested in "normal life." She wanted a life focused on spirituality and learning. She invited us into her life and described her rituals each day, which involved waking up before sunrise to pray and garden. She studied, read, and meditated throughout the day. She also provided counseling to the people in the area for their daily challenges and supervised new students who wanted to become monks.

Owing to this experience, my appreciation and understanding of a Buddhist temple is now completely different. I had been to dozens of Buddhist temples before with skilled tour guides, but this was a totally different experience. I reached out and got to experience the Buddhist faith in a way that wouldn't have been possible by just touring a temple. Now when I walk into a Buddhist temple, I can really *feel* the site and understand its deep spiritual context. I also learned that Buddhists are generally open and welcoming to outsiders joining in their rituals.

Because of this experience, today I encourage travelers to try to arrange a Q&A session with a monastic, priest, imam, or rabbi (or ask their travel company to arrange a meeting). Religious clergy are often happy to host groups and answer questions and are used to fielding difficult questions. But by meeting with someone dedicated to the faith, you have an opportunity to see religious practice through someone else's perspective—and that is an experience guaranteed to make you see religious sites with new eyes.

Attend a Religious Service, Holiday, or Festival

I always find it fascinating to attend a religious service (if one is open to the public). However, if you do not feel comfortable doing so, or if no public service is available, check the calendar or ask some locals if there are any religious celebrations or festivals you can join. Religious holidays are often less threatening for first-time visitors and can be a great way to connect with people of different faiths.

In June 2019, I had dinner with my Turkish friends Berna and Onur, and they told me about one of their most impactful travel experiences. While they were visiting a friend in Spain, their friend told them, "You've come at the perfect time."

It was time for the Romería de El Rocío pilgrimage (held just an hour's drive from Seville). The small town numbers fewer than 1,000 residents, and its streets are mostly unpaved gravel or dirt; but every year, this Catholic celebration of the Virgin of El Rocío transforms the small town, as almost half a million people flock there to participate in the procession marking the second day of Pentecost. As Berna and Onur recalled, women wore traditional flamenco dresses and men wore cordovan hats, short jackets, and riding pants. Some pilgrims arrived in horses and carriages. Carrying candles, the devotees walked to the churches, the candles flickering in the night sky like stars. They were playing music, singing about the Virgin Mary, and praying.

Looking back, Berna and Onur ranked this festival as one of the best travel experiences they'd ever had. Even though they had been raised Muslim, they were moved and affected by the Catholic festival, and by talking to the pilgrims who had come from all over Spain for the celebration.

As Berna and Onur's story shows, attending religious services can be a beautiful and moving educational experience, which can deepen one's appreciation for other faiths. Your intent in participating in a religious service abroad is probably not to reconsider your belief system. But learning more about the religions of other cultures is important for understanding the emotional and spiritual life of others.

During Ramadan in Washington, DC, I commonly meet Christians, Jews, and atheists attending *iftar* dinners. They wait for food with the Muslims, asking questions about the tradition, making sure that they don't inadvertently do anything disrespectful toward the Muslims attending. These people don't come because they are practicing Islam; they come as friends. Most are respectful and don't eat or drink before the call to prayer.

These types of exchanges are important; I've similarly had many Muslim and Christian friends who have attended Shabbat dinners with Jewish friends. Meals and holidays are fun and a great way to connect with others.

Filiz, another friend of mine, whose family is from Turkey and who also grew up in a Muslim family, told me about her experiences of connecting with other people's rituals. She told me that as a child, she had wanted to celebrate Christmas. She grew up in the United States, and all her friends had Christmas trees; it was all they talked about at school every December. She wanted to experience this event that everyone spoke about, but because she was Muslim, her father would not allow her to put up a Christmas tree in the house. She would, however, smuggle a very small Christmas tree into her home. Her mother became complicit in her rebellion and would help her hide it. She would then excitedly, but secretly, decorate the tiny branches of the tree.

I laughed hearing Filiz's story; as I told her, when I was about 16 or 17 years old, I had a similar experience. I thought the Christmas tree looked really cool and was curious about it. So I went out and found a small tree; it wasn't a Christmas tree, but basically a fallen branch of a pine tree. I brought it back home and erected the tiny tree in our home and called it a Christmas tree.

I'm lucky to have a mother who is open to other cultures. She's deeply religious, a conservative Muslim, but she is not threatened by other people's faiths and does not mind being exposed to them. My dad, on the other hand, was not so thrilled to come home and see a makeshift replica of a Christmas tree in his home.

"Why is this branch here?" he asked me. "This is our Christmas tree," I gleefully told him. "But we are Muslim," he responded. I retorted simply, "Yes, I know. But it's Christmas!"

"Christmas is for Christians," my father said. "But wasn't Jesus a Muslim prophet?" I retorted (very proud of myself for the comeback). My father looked at me with his typical about-to-argue-with-me face, but he decided it wasn't worth the effort; my mom's taking my side also pressured him to back down. "Fine. Keep the tree. But don't go around telling people we have a Christmas tree in our house," he said.

We are all curious about other people's identities, religions, rituals, and cultures. Expressing this curiosity to friends or locals while traveling, or joining in a local holiday or religious festival, is a great way to learn about someone else's life. Participating in someone else's ritual is a lot more real and intimate than just visiting a cathedral or mosque, where the architecture is impressive but the human meaning behind the site is often missing.

We all have different practices. Most Muslims, for instance, do not sing in their mosques. But in a church, singing echoes throughout the walls. That's what makes these experiences unique. In some cases, the differences might make us feel a bit uncomfortable, but it's this lack of comfort that helps create a meaningful experience and embodies the heart of exploration and travel.

Exploring Religious Traditions

Regardless of your beliefs regarding religion, we should all consider exploring, and even participating in, the rituals of others. It is perhaps one of the most difficult forms of travel (since religious beliefs are such a strong part of our identities). There is something unique and important about joining a religious service, even when you don't speak the language or share the same faith. Taking part in these events teaches us respect and tolerance. It might be hard when we encounter traditions we disagree with, but it also creates an opportunity for a respectful conversation.

I suggest that these types of religious exploration can begin with a few important steps:

- Suspend judgment.
- Approach other faiths with a spirit of humility, respect, and learning.
- Ask if a priest, pastor, imam, rabbi, or monastic is willing to engage in a Q&A session, or ask your travel company to arrange a meeting for your group.
- Invite a friend of a different faith to your holiday services, celebrations, or meals (a Christmas or Easter service, a Ramadan *iftar*, a Shabbat or Passover dinner), or ask a friend if you can attend one of his or her services.
- Ask locals if there is a religious service or festival you can attend.

Importantly, joining others' rituals can also be a way to unite people in the face of growing xenophobia. Showing the world that we can coexist and not see others' practices as a threat to our own is the only way to create peace between different cultures. As travelers, we can lead the way, by demonstrating how learning about or attending another faith's religious services can be a powerful experience.

As religious divides grow around the world, I am always inspired by acts that show coexistence and tolerance, even in the least likely places. In various Arab countries (including Jordan,

Lebanon, and Palestine), Christians stand in the streets during Ramadan, giving water and dates to Muslims stuck in traffic who can't make it home on time to break their fasts.

In June 2019, Christians, Yazidis, and Shabaks in Iraq distributed roses to Muslims for the Muslim holiday Eid al-Fitr (celebrating the end of Ramadan).[1] A few months earlier, young Iraqi Muslims in Mosul helped clean and restore the church of Saint Thomas the Apostle, which had been ransacked, damaged, and used as a prison by ISIS. The young Iraqi Muslims also joined their Christian neighbors in attending Mass.

We don't always have to travel far to experience other faiths, because in most places in the world you can find unique rituals right next door. In the United States, Jews and Muslims have started encouraging neighbors to visit synagogues and mosques, meet with them, and learn about their traditions as a way to counter anti-Semitism and Islamophobia. All you have to do is call and let the mosque or temple know you are coming, so that you can discuss what activities would be appropriate for you to attend.

These programs—which I would argue are a form of travel—are important for building bridges in our divided world. In a similar way, tourism can be an opportunity to build bridges, learn about other faiths, and participate in interfaith exchanges. By connecting to the human side of the impressive religious monuments that appear on most travel top-10 lists, we can contribute to improving religious understanding both in our own communities and in the communities we visit.

CHAPTER 11

REVISITING
HISTORICAL NARRATIVES

WE OFTEN THINK about history from a one-sided perspective, remembering what we've learned in school, read in a textbook, or seen in a movie. But the moment you begin to see history from another person's perspective, it can be transformational. While the past consists of historical facts, our narratives about those facts change. As we travel, it is important that we seek to learn the historical facts, but also understand the narratives based on these facts in each destination we visit.

Don't Always Believe
the Guidebook (or the Guide)

I have always been fascinated by Greek mythology and history. I grew up just 40 miles from Jaffa, where in legend Perseus used Medusa's head to turn the sea monster into stone and set Andromeda free from the monster. I have always wanted to visit Crete because it's the birthplace of Zeus, and to see Knossos,

which has almost 9,000 years of history. When I told my colleagues in Athens about my plans to visit Crete in September
2019, they referred me to Ioanna, who they said was the best
tour guide on the island.

Ioanna seemed to know everyone in Heraklion, the main
city in Crete. We started our day by visiting the Heraklion Museum to learn about the Minoan civilization. Afterward, we continued to Knossos, where I learned about the religious practices
and mythological stories connected to the site, such as Theseus
killing the Minotaur (a half-human and half-bull creature).

Eventually, we arrived at a building where we could hear
other tour guides talking about "the king's room" and "the
queen's room" and the importance of this palace to the Minoans.
I was excited to learn about the king and queen who had lived
there. But Ioanna was quick to urge caution. "We have no proof
that there was really a palace here, and the 'king's and queen's
rooms' are heavily reconstructed" to look as they do today.

"But the tour guides said that there was a palace," I argued.
Ioanna patiently explained why this was the case: "This is what
[the British archaeologist] Sir Arthur John Evans said when he
first excavated the site in the early 1900s, but these findings are
now contested by many archaeologists."

Later in the evening, I brought up these debates when we
met with archaeologist Don Evely, the former curator of the British School at Athens (BSA) at Knossos Palace, and Mihalis Papa-
giannakis, the antiquities curator of the Archaeological Museum
of Heraklion. Both of them agreed with Ioanna's assessment that
we don't really know that a king and queen lived there. Dr. Pa-
pagiannakis said that we also have to remember that Evans grew
up with Homer's writings, which influenced his worldview when
he was excavating.

Despite what we know (and don't know) about Knossos,
many tour guides and even travel publications refer to the com-

plex as a palace where a king and a queen lived. The story of a king and queen is captivating, and abandoning such a narrative is not easy. Tour guides often tease each other by saying, "Why spoil a good story with facts?"

Not everything a tour guide tells you is factual. Not everything you read on a sign (even at a museum) is accurate. Travel books are especially notorious for recounting popular myths at the expense of facts. As we travel, we must therefore be aware that we will encounter a lot of misinformation, and be cautious about accepting a story told by a guide as absolute fact.

I view travel as a window that encourages us to view different perspectives, and it should prompt us to ask further questions, research, read, and pursue the facts wherever they take us. I remember traveling to Oman with archaeologists Chris Thornton and Jeffrey Rose. When we visited Bat, a United Nations World Heritage site that Dr. Thornton had excavated, he would often respond to my many questions about the beehive tombs of Bat by saying, "We still don't know." Bat is one of the most important archaeological sites in Oman, and both Dr. Thornton and Dr. Rose refused to spread unsupported theories and assumptions about the tombs. However, a tour guide we hired had no problem telling us all about the tombs, their history, the rituals used in the burials, the architecture and what it meant about the afterlife, and even stories about the political system of the people who built the tombs. None of these stories were based on facts, but they were more fulfilling for tourists to hear than "We are still researching and excavating, and we don't know the answers yet."

The king's and queen's rooms and tombs at Bat illustrate a growing problem around the world: "tourist archaeology," or the commercialization of archaeological sites for popular consumption. Sites with good stories and big monuments sell; they attract crowds and funding, but also generate misinformation.

As we travel, we have to prepare ourselves and read about the destinations we are traveling to before and after the trip. Traveling is not about passively accepting information—it is an opportunity to think critically and learn. We will be told much factual information and many true stories, but we will also be told half-truths and nonfactual stories.

On one of the tours to the Holy Land that I was leading, I did an experiment with the group. We decided that I would purposely say nonfactual things throughout the day and see if the group could catch them. I talked about the (fictional) use of elephants in the siege of Masada and said that Mount Scopus in Jerusalem (Mount Lookout) was named for the Latin for "mouthwash." We wanted to see how long it would take before the group would stop believing everything I said just because I was the tour guide. Eventually, when my "alternative facts" became outrageous, they called me on it and we shared a good laugh.

All of us should travel with an open mind, but we should also be willing to reassess our knowledge, learn about new things, and hear from experts. Don't be a passive consumer of information!

Understand That History Is Not Just about the Past

Like everyone else, I grew up watching American-produced Vietnam War movies. It was always the good guys (the Americans) versus the bad guys (the Vietcong), with Arnold Schwarzenegger–style action that gave the viewer no choice but to fervently cheer for the USA. Despite the fact that I grew up in Palestine, the movies were enough to suck me into a tangle of misconceptions and biases regarding the war.

When I decided to visit Vietnam, I began learning some different perspectives. Before the trip, I started reading and watching documentaries about Vietnam's history. I binge-watched the Ken Burns and Lynn Novick documentary about the Vietnam War and was amazed by the different narratives and my ignorance about the topic. Beyond good guys and bad buys, the American narrative had been that Vietnam would be a foothold for communism in Asia and that it would create a domino effect in neighboring countries. The rest of Asia would eventually transform into communist regimes, controlled by China and Russia. There had also been a strong antiwar movement in the United States, with many students and activists joining demonstrations against the war.

Talking to Americans about Vietnam, I further realized that there were strong emotions tied up in the history of the war. I realized how painful revisiting history could be. I remember sitting with a former US federal judge over lunch and talking to him about visiting Vietnam. He said, "I could never go there because of how they treated our prisoners of war. I just can't." Confronting these memories is painful, and being willing to hear a narrative of history that conflicts with your own can be troubling.

When I finally traveled to Vietnam, I heard completely different perspectives. Listening to the stories of the "bad guys" (ex-Vietcong and Viet Minh fighters) from American films, I heard a narrative of liberation. For these Vietnamese soldiers, the war had little to do with communism and everything to do with their achieving the independence of their country. Political independence overshadowed any larger communist program.

In Saigon, for instance, our group met with Bay Hon and Chin Naghia, two former guerrilla fighters who were in their 20s when they joined the Vietcong and led the attack on the Independence Palace in 1968 as part of the Tet Offensive.

Chin was shot and badly injured, and eventually the group was arrested. They told us how they were awaiting execution by the South Vietnamese government when the US military intervened, due to fears that their execution would lead to reprisal killings of American POWs by the North Vietnamese.

A conversation started between the American group and the Vietnamese; individuals who had been on opposite sides of the war and history listened to each other's stories.

As Chin told the group, "It made me feel so much better to know that there were so many Americans who were protesting against the war. Knowing that not all Americans were supportive of the war was an important moment for me, because then I realized I couldn't hate Americans."

She continued, "I wanted you to know that I respect American mothers who sacrificed their sons. I respect the soldiers. My anger is not toward the soldiers, it is only for people who made the war. I respect the mother who had to send her kids into this crazy war.

"I hope you understand," she added. "I had to fight for my country. It's not personal. You would have done the same thing if your country was attacked. It's not against you. I hope we can learn from this, so we never have war again and we can work together instead."

It was emotional, and there were a lot of tears and hugs; every group I brought left in tears. There were also many important takeaways from the conversation. I was struck by how history was more than just dates and figures: in both Vietnam and the United States, history had emotional and personal importance, and was part of complex narratives about national identity.

I was also impressed by how one event in history could have so many complex causes and outcomes and how it could be seen in different ways. Neither the American community nor the Vietnamese had all thought the same way about the war (we met other Vietnamese in the south who had strongly hoped for an American victory and had spent years as refugees after the fall of Saigon).

During another tour I led in Vietnam, we met with Nguyen Hong My, a Vietnamese pilot who had been the first to shoot down an American plane in 1972. Nguyen received his training in the Soviet Union, where he learned how to fly a MiG-21; during his service, he shot down two American planes. Ultimately, his plane was downed by an American pilot; he parachuted out and survived but broke both arms.

Nguyen told us his unlikely story of reconciliation. In 2007, he was visited by the American pilot Daniel Edwards Cherry, who had shot down Nguyen's plane in 1972. I remember Nguyen talking to our group about the encounter and saying, "Once we met as enemies, but now we met as friends." About a year later, Nguyen met with John Stiles, another American pilot. This time, the situation was reversed: Nguyen was the pilot who had shot down Stiles's plane during the war. These men had met on the battlefield as enemies and tried to kill each other in the skies over Vietnam. But both were willing to rethink the past and overcome their enmity in order to form a friendship with each other.

As we sat in a circle outside a coffee shop next to the wreckage of a B-52 that had crashed in Hanoi, we listened to Nguyen's stories and examined the photos he had brought with him. My American tourist group—one of whom had spent most of his career working with American Vietnam War veterans—sat, listened, and asked questions.

Hearing stories that conflict with our own historical narratives should not be seen as a threat to our story and identity. Perhaps one of the worst things to come from the Enlightenment was the idea that conflicting stories can't exist side by side. But in many cultures around the world (and in many biblical narratives, including the four Gospels), different narratives are welcomed. They give us different perspectives.

While the perspectives and narratives of these American tourists were challenged, they did not walk out of the discussions with the idea that it was the American side that was evil and the Vietnamese instead were the good guys. This is not the point of revisiting history. Both sides learned from each other and realized that there is a multiplicity of experiences. Both sides had reasons to question their own narrative and learn about the narrative of the other.

We also met with a Vietnamese historian on the tour. He said something that stuck with us long after we left the country. One of the travelers asked, "How do the Vietnamese feel about Americans after the war?" The historian's answer was unexpected.

For almost 1,000 years, Vietnam was occupied by China, and for 100 years Vietnam was occupied by France. Vietnam was also occupied by Japan during World War II. After the United States, Vietnam had another war with China and a war with Cambodia. As the historian concluded, Vietnam's war with the United States was not the most defining part of its history; that war actually represents a very small part.

There is a reason the why the Vietnamese now emphasize historical conflicts with China over the conflict with Americans. Today, the United States has become an important ally for Vietnam, as Vietnam and China are embroiled in territorial disputes in the South China Sea. In other words, history is not just about the past: it is very much about present concerns and conflicts. And depending on current events, we emphasize or silence events in our history to create certain narratives about the present.

Overall, when traveling, it is therefore important to remember that history is also about emotions, identities, and current events (among other things), so we need to think critically about the histories we hear. We miss out on so much if we travel to Vietnam and understand its history only from an American history book. The Vietnamese historical accounts are equally colored by the lenses of national and personal narratives. In other words, no narrative has a monopoly on truth and facts.

Consider How the Community
Has Built Its Narrative

"Have you learned about one of the biggest wars in the Americas?" asked Vivian Gunsett. I had sat down with Vivian after a talk I gave in Asunción, Paraguay; it was my first visit to the country.

Sometimes traveling makes us realize how little we know about the history of the places we visit, and even if we know the history, it can show us how little we understand the long-term consequences of historical events.

I had spoken at an event for National Geographic Learning, and after my talk, I asked the audience if anyone would like to join me for dinner or drinks. I do this at almost every event because I feel it's wrong for me to speak and walk out without opening a conversation with attendees. I am there to speak, but also to learn. So about a dozen people joined me at a local pub, and we started talking about Paraguay, its history, its current challenges, and its future.

This was when Vivian and others started asking me about my knowledge of Paraguay's history. "I am sure you've heard about the 1864 war? We still feel the pain and the consequences of this war," Vivian said. I admitted that I didn't know anything about it.

She went on to explain the war and its aftermath. In Asunción, they feel that the Paraguayan War, also known as the War of the Triple Alliance, still affects them today—even though the war was almost 160 years ago. The magnitude of the fighting was astonishing; the conflict pitted Brazil, Uruguay, and Argentina against Paraguay. The war lasted six years, and 60 percent of the Paraguayan population was killed. Some sources estimate that following the war, only 28,000 men in Paraguay remained—compared with 100,000 women and more than 80,000 children.

Vivian told me that she grew up hearing her father talk about the war, and it had become part of her identity. "I feel a deep sense of gratitude toward Paraguayans who fought and rebuilt our country," she said.

"Travelers to Paraguay rarely get to learn about the war and its aftermath on the people. . . . Men and women gave up their possessions to pay for war. Women gave up their children, who fought and died because there were no more men to fight," Vivian said. "The few that remained, especially women, had a lot of responsibility to rebuild the country. Sixty years after the devastating war, we had another territorial dispute with Bolivia, a country that was left without any access to the sea or a river that goes to the sea." She concluded, "In the two wars, Paraguay lost land but remains free and independent."

The group of Paraguayans then debated whether the government should develop tourist sites to teach about the war. My friend Ana said she would prefer to show tourists the beautiful places and traditions in the country. Another Paraguayan, named Rita, disagreed. "But I want travelers to know the magnitude of what we have achieved as a nation despite the horrific history, but also to imagine what we could have been if they had not stolen our land, our people, and our country. It is important they understand the bravery of our people. The sense of loss is present in every Paraguayan."

Luis, another participant in the conversation, summed up his view. "Paraguay is like a phoenix resurrected from the ashes. Our courage and perseverance creates a sense of pride and admiration for our country."

Despite the magnitude of the war, very few people outside of Paraguay have heard about it. I asked my friends in Brazil and Argentina if they'd heard of the war, and even they knew very little about it. "It was 160 years ago," one said. "I don't know much about it." Most told me they had studied it in school but it wasn't a major focus, and they didn't know that it was still a big deal for Paraguayans.

But in Paraguay, the war is still in the hearts and minds of the population. Individuals grow up with the war being a central component of their identity and history. When Paraguayans speak about the war, it's not a war that happened 160 years ago; it's as if they had lived through it themselves.

As the Paraguayan War illustrates, historical events are remembered or forgotten based on how they relate to current events and concepts of self. A nation's stories about the past constitute a living morality tale about "who we are," "where we come from," and "where we're going."

As a result, when learning about a country's history for the first time, it is important to consider how the present intersects with the past. How does an archaeological site, museum display, or historical event fit into the group's narrative of who they are? Who curates and promotes this narrative (the government, a majority ethnic group)? What historical events or groups are silenced in (or left out of) the narrative or museum display, because their inclusion might challenge the moral of the story? Which groups are "othered" by the narrative, or set up as enemies or threats to the group's way of life? These are just a few of the questions that can help ascertain how the story or display contributes to collective memory and self-fashioning.

Be Attuned to Different Pasts

Many of the histories we hear while traveling are part of national narratives; museums are funded by governments, and archaeological sites are woven into stories about the nation. These stories are important to learn, because they tell us about how the community envisions itself: who is part of "us" and who is "other."

These narratives are important to hear, but they also should be handled with care. States and nations are anachronistically projected into the past, and archaeological sites are preserved or demolished based on how they fit into our communal myths. In the Middle East, for instance, it has been common practice for years to destroy Byzantine, Sassanid, and Ottoman sites in order to get to Phoenician, Pharaonic, or ancient Israelite sites underneath (sites that better champion communal claims based on ethnic nationalism).

As a result, I always challenge travelers to think critically about history. Whether you are visiting a site for the first time or revisiting well-known sites, reading different perspectives reveals how history is alive and contested. So the next time you travel, try investigating "new pasts" in addition to new places:

- Before you travel, try to read a book, watch a documentary, or listen to some podcasts or audiobooks on the history of the place you will be visiting.

- Search out different perspectives on historical events. Explore familiar narratives from a new angle (with books like *Those Damned Rebels: The American Revolution as Seen Through British Eyes*), or look for multivocal histories (like *Side by Side: Parallel Histories of Israel-Palestine*).[1]

- Try hiring a few guides throughout the trip, to hear some different perspectives (and don't be afraid to ask the guides questions).

- Don't trust everything you read in a guidebook or see on a museum sign, and don't take as gospel every story the guide tells you. Instead, understand that these are just different narratives, which may or may not be based in fact.

- Be aware that a lot of archaeology is speculative, and there are debates about the purpose, usage, and cultural importance of sites. Ask your guide what debates exist about the heritage site you are visiting.

- Consider the elements of the story you are hearing. What events does the story highlight, and what events are left out? What parts of the narrative do locals consider emotionally important, or important for the community's identity? What does the story or site say about how the community views itself? What does the story or site suggest about who the community sees as the "other" or outsiders?

Travel is an opportunity for us to learn about history not just from a textbook but to emotionally understand why certain pasts are important to the communities we visit. Visiting Vietnam and Paraguay, for instance, brought textbook history to life for me, challenged what I'd learned from the media, and illustrated how history is embodied in individual and collective narratives of self.

CHAPTER 12

RESOLVING CONFLICT AND THE ART OF RESPONSIBLE TRAVEL

"WHY SHOULD I 'travel responsibly'? It takes time and money; I don't want to think, I don't want to talk to people—I'd rather just relax and enjoy the beach!"

I have a very introverted friend who, when she speaks, says exactly what she's thinking—and I appreciate it! Because if one person is thinking it, there are probably others thinking it too. We have busy lives: the demands of our jobs, homes, and families often make us see vacation as an easy way out of the daily grind of responsibility.

But when we travel, we still have a responsibility: a moral responsibility to first do no harm to the communities we visit. If all our money is going to international hotel chains, cruise companies, and travel companies, the chances are that only pennies are reaching the communities we are visiting.

Beyond this moral responsibility, changing the way we travel also improves our travel experience. We see new things, taste new things, and experience new things; we build a future where we don't have to spend our vacation elbowing our way through overcrowded heritage sites; we have a more relaxing vacation; and we walk away with more than just the same Instagram photo that everyone else has.

Consider this: I've been to more than 60 countries and stayed in everything from two-star hotels to five- and the self-declared six-star hotels all over the world. But one of the best hotels I've ever visited was a locally run, environmentally friendly, vegan hotel in the jungles of Indonesia. As a Middle Easterner, I was not excited about hearing that the hotel restaurant had no meat or cheese. But I had what turned out to be one of the best meals of my life, which also inspired me to eat more vegetarian food. Overall, it was also one of the best hotel rooms I've ever stayed in, at a reasonable price—and an unforgettable experience.

I say this to emphasize that responsible travel does not have to be an either/or choice between fun and sustainability. It does not have to be more expensive (local boutique hotels are often priced reasonably). It does not have to be more time-consuming; you can follow a few of the tips at the end of each chapter, or just hire a company to plan a responsible travel package for you by perusing the B Corp website's travel listings.[1]

If you're an introvert, you don't have to talk to everyone—just focus on some of the other target areas I've recommended, like participating in educational activities, being more environmentally friendly, or supporting community projects. And you can still spend time at the beach or the pool. In short, responsible travel is not a zero-sum game: you do not have to lose something to make sure that locals are benefiting. Responsible travel benefits everyone!

Responsible travel will look a little different for each of us. A person's travel experiences will vary widely depending on the person's means, skin color, gender, personality, nationality, and language spoken. But each of us can find ways to improve travel for ourselves, for others, and for the communities we visit.

To take into account these different travel styles, this book has provided tips and strategies—some quick and easy, some more difficult—for how to make your travel more responsible (and more fun!). Here are a few final thoughts on how we can transform our travel experiences—and in doing so, transform the world.

Don't Be Afraid to Ask the Hard Questions

Like my introverted friend (who expressed her suspicions about whether sustainable travel would require more money, more effort, and more socializing), you can improve your travel by being honest and being willing to ask difficult questions.

Once, during one of our tours in Israel and Palestine, our group of MEJDI travelers met with Mazen, a Palestinian refugee who lived in Deheisheh refugee camp (in the Bethlehem district of the West Bank). Mazen spoke about his life, and how his family and thousands of other Palestinians in the camp had been displaced, expelled from their homes as a result of the creation of Israel.

When Mazen was finished speaking, one of the travelers raised his hand and asked a question. "I don't get it," he said. "Why don't you just work harder and get yourself out of the refugee camp? Move on."

This was the beginning of a conflict: a clash of ideas. But as insensitive as the question was, not all conflicts are bad. Sometimes conflicts can be used to open conversations, and sometimes a lack of conflict implies a lack of freedom (or willingness) to express ourselves openly.

Anytime humans interact, disagreements and conflicts are guaranteed. Whether it is between our families, friends, neighbors, or strangers, we will encounter conflict. It's how we handle those conflicts that matters.

Mazen was not offended by the question posed to him by the traveler, and he used the question to explain more about the reality of life in a refugee camp. He explained that most people didn't have the financial means to leave the camp. The unemployment rate in the Bethlehem district in 2018 stood at 21 percent (and in the camp the numbers were higher).[2] Many of the residents (including Mazen) were in Israeli prisons as teenagers and never finished high school. For the next half hour, Mazen and the traveler engaged in a tough conversation about the Palestinian refugee situation.

The question this man asked Mazen was phrased offensively, but it raised questions that others might have been too embarrassed to ask, and Mazen used the question to prompt an honest conversation. It opened a window for both the traveler and the refugee to learn about each other's world and perspective.

Having a conflict with someone doesn't mean we have to become enemies; enmity is born from our inability to manage our conflicts, listen to one another, express ourselves in a respectful way, and tolerate disagreement and diverse opinions.

So let's not be afraid to ask hard questions; and let's learn to have more productive conflicts—especially when they involve competing ideas. Uncomfortable situations and interpersonal disagreements can help us reexamine our own values and beliefs, and open up important conversations.

Strive to Suspend Judgment and Understand Other Perspectives

In 2015, I was on a speaking tour in Japan. I had been invited to speak to an auditorium of almost 1,000 students at a local university and was eager to talk to them about the role of education in peace building and what they could do to advance peace in the world.

But halfway through my talk, I was ready to give up. I had made a few jokes; usually my jokes got loud laughs from audiences—but not at this university. I tried shifting gears and talked about some emotional situations I'd faced—but the audience didn't give me even the slightest frown or sympathetic groan. I tried some interactive approaches, like asking questions and trying to get the audience to participate—but it made no difference. I started telling myself that those students must have hated me as a speaker.

The following day, I met with the professor who had invited me. He had collected hundreds of feedback papers from the students who attended my talk. As he shuffled through them, I was terrified when he suggested that we take a look and read some together. I expected the comments to be vicious.

I was wrong.

The feedback was full of compliments and kind words, and the students expressed strong interest in conflict resolution and peacemaking. I was puzzled. I asked the professor why it seemed that the students had been so uninterested in my talk.

"It's a cultural thing," he responded. "In Japan, at events like this you are not supposed to draw attention to yourself as an attendee. You don't want to create a distraction. The focus should be on the speaker. You listen and learn without drawing any attention to yourself."

In their essay "Conflict Resolution in Intercultural Settings," in *Conflict Resolution Theory and Practice*, Kevin Avruch and Peter W. Black write that culture provides "the 'lens' by which we view and bring into focus our world; the 'logic' (known as common sense) by which we order it; the 'grammar' by which it makes sense."[3]

In other words, while certain things (like laughing at a speaker's jokes) might seem obvious or common sense to us, it is important to remember that these things are not common sense at all—they are often part of a cultural lens through which we view the world. These cultural differences can generate conflict or emotional distress because we are not aware of or do not understand the different sets of rules and values that other cultures have. As a result, intercultural communication is a challenge, because we all bring our own set of rules, expectations, values, and beliefs to the table. When we travel or communicate with other cultures, these "grammars" often clash with the grammars of our travel companions, local communities, or other tourists we encounter along the way; and this can create discomfort and even conflict.

Being aware that we speak different cultural languages (as well as different languages) is vital for becoming responsible travelers. We are likely to encounter things we don't understand or don't agree with. But if we determine not to take these differences personally, and approach these differences with respect and a spirit of learning, diversity can be a source of joy rather than pain.

I judged these students because I didn't understand their culture. I assumed they didn't care, and I was very wrong. I was in their country and expecting them to follow the cultural norms I was used to. It was ignorant of me to expect that. All cultures are different—all people are different (even if they're from the same culture!)—our expectations, communication styles, needs, histories, and experiences are not all the same.

Yet it's easy to make the mistake of assuming that cultural norms will be similar to ours wherever we travel. If we are not used to tipping in restaurants, we feel ripped off when expected to tip. We get upset when the service style at hotels and restaurants is not as warm and friendly as we're used to. We assume that we are being disrespected or even personally attacked by new ideas or customs. But it is unrealistic for us to arrive at a new destination and expect all the norms and rules to be identical to ours—that is not traveling at all. We might not agree with or like certain practices, but we are guests in these destinations and must check our sense of cultural privilege (or rightness) at the door.

In the travel industry, for instance, I often find myself facing different cultures of service from one country to another. At one point, I worked with a hotel in Oman and felt very frustrated about the slow responses. Even though Omanis are also Arab and speak Arabic, I couldn't understand them. Everything took longer than I was used to: email responses and confirmations took days or weeks. This is not to say that Oman doesn't excel in customer service. However, their focus is more relational than punctual. I needed to understand that and learn how to work with local cultural norms. And in the end, Oman's relaxed atmosphere is one of the things that make it a great destination to visit.

Relinquish Privilege

During one of our tours in Israel and Palestine, we were headed to Sderot (in southern Israel) after visiting the West Bank city of Hebron, a flashpoint of tensions between Israeli settlers and Palestinians. I was leading a group of 36 American students and professors, who were on a study abroad program focused on conflict and religious studies. Shira Nesher, an Israeli peacemaker and former guide for the Israeli Army, was co-guiding with me.

Approaching the Tarqumiyah checkpoint, which serves as the main passage for products from Israel to enter the southern part of the West Bank, we weren't expecting any issues. Our group had already passed multiple checkpoints and had no problems.

But when we tried to pass, our bus driver (a Palestinian from Jerusalem) was told by the soldiers to park the bus and get off to undergo extra security checks. As I was the only other Palestinian on the bus, the soldiers soon told me to join the driver.

I didn't want to create an argument with them about the absurdity of the situation. (It was rather pointless to check the driver and me but not the rest of the bus—especially since we had access to the luggage.) But I didn't say anything. I just wanted us to pass quickly and get to our next meeting on time.

However, Shira, our Israeli guide, decided to ask the soldiers about the reasoning behind this selective treatment. Her question of "why" was met matter-of-factly:

Security: "We need to check Aziz and Mustafa [the driver]."

He turned to me and Mustafa. "Both of you, take off your shoes, jackets, and belts; bring your backpacks . . ."

Equally matter-of-factly, Shira replied, "OK"—and started taking off her shoes and belt, trailing behind us.

Security: "What do you think you are doing?"

Shira: "I am going through the same security checks they are going through."

Security: "What reality are you living in?" Suddenly realizing that she was protesting his profiling us for being Palestinian, he said, "You wouldn't have done this if you were in a New York airport and the security pulled a Muslim guy in front of you for extra checking, would you?"

Shira: "My reality is different than your reality. These are not strangers in the airport. They are my coworkers. I didn't ask you not to check them; I will not interfere with your work. However, you should check me too. I don't accept you racially profiling my colleagues. We are one team; we spend 15 hours together every day. We work together, eat together, and at checkpoints we should be treated similarly. We are equal in everything we do—why not here?"

Shira then underwent the same security checks that Mustafa and I underwent. She didn't get angry; she just used a calm voice to force the security officer to reconsider his actions. She could have yelled and tossed about accusations, which would have surely made him angry, but she chose a different path. She decided to create cognitive dissonance and prompt him to rethink the objectives and practices of his work. And she showed him that she considered Palestinians her equals.

What impressed me was that Shira didn't just demand better treatment of Palestinians from afar or sermonize about justice and equality. Instead, when she realized she couldn't guarantee that her Palestinian colleagues would be treated equally, she gave up her privileges in a show of equality.

When we returned to the bus, one of the Christian theology professors told us in a trembling voice, "When I saw the soldiers profiling you, I was angry. All of us on the bus were angry. But Shira, you showed us how to use love and respect to model a different reality. I have to tell you, to me, that embodies the biblical commandment to love your neighbor."

Shira also provided a great example of how as travelers we must be aware of the privileges we enjoy because of our nationality, economic class, race, ethnicity, gender, skin color, and religion. As a male, I have the freedom to not worry about certain things women have to consider while traveling; and as a Palestinian Arab, I can move more freely and blend in while traveling in South America and the Middle East, but I often become a target of suspicion in parts of Europe and North America.

In other words, being aware of our privileges will help us consider them as we communicate and engage with other groups. Like Shira, as travelers we must always assess our privileges. In the end, the power we possess having the means to travel internationally is a luxury, and we must be reflective about how these privileges divide us from or connect us to those around us.

Be Kind toward Others

I met Arno, a former neo-Nazi, while moderating an event in New York City. Arno was one of the speakers on our panel; during his presentation, he shared how he had become a white suprem-acist at age 16—and the encounter that had made him change his mind. He had grown up angry, a teen in an alcoholic home where emotional abuse was the norm. He had reacted by bullying other kids and committing acts of vandalism.

In school, he fell in with a group of kids who believed that Jews were bringing Latinos and black people to America on pur-pose to destroy the white race; he said, "I joined up for the kicks and to make people angry." He ultimately dropped out of high school and made a meager income working at a T-shirt store. His money went to buying alcohol. Six days a week he would eat only packaged ramen noodles; once a week he treated himself to McDonald's.

But the fast food restaurant turned out to be the place that began a shift in Arno's perspective. Behind the register, an elderly African American woman would always greet him "with a smile as warm and unconditional as the sun."[4] Arno didn't like that the woman was welcoming and nice to him—it challenged every-thing he believed in. It bothered him so much that he would leave McDonald's and immediately try to get into a fight so that he could maintain his worldview of besiegement.

One day, Arno decided to get a swastika tattoo on his middle finger to provoke people. But as his weekly trip to McDonald's approached, he found himself thinking, "I don't want to show my swastika to the nice elderly black lady." He had been affected by her without even realizing it.

As much as he tried to hide the tattoo, she noticed it. She saw the swastika and froze. "What is this?" she asked. While nor-mally Arno would respond by picking a fight, this time a wave of shame swept over him; he couldn't even look the woman in the eyes. He muttered, "Nothing." She softly responded, "You're a better person than that. That's not who you are."

Even though Arno didn't leave the neo-Nazi group right away, he said it was this seed of compassion that spread doubt in his mind about the doctrines of white supremacy. In the end, that woman became one of the reasons why he decided to leave the neo-Nazis. While others he encountered spewed hate, this African American woman's kindness moved him. In retrospect, Arno describes these kinds of people as peace warriors: individuals who brought love into his life until there was no longer any room for hatred.

Arno's story is a powerful example of how a kind word can make a difference in someone's life. While traveling, we will encounter angry people, rude people, racist people, people who will offend us, and people who act unjustly toward us. But I've learned from Arno to always act with kindness and compassion, and to always try to smile. Most times, we will never know how our kindness affects others; but as Arno's story shows, unconditional kindness—even in a moment's exchange between a service worker and a customer—can change even the hardest of hearts.

Share a Cup of Coffee

A final story I want to leave you with is about coffee. Coffee is an essential drink in the Middle East. But its value goes beyond its high caffeine content and its strong taste, as we slowly sip it from the *finjan* (special small coffee cup). Research shows that Arabs were among the first to drink coffee, in the 15th century. Within a hundred years it found its way to every corner of the world, including the New World, which eventually became a leader in coffee production.

I grew up learning about coffee's symbolic power in our community. The acceptance of a marriage proposal is sealed by drinking coffee. A wedding is celebrated by drinking coffee. When you offer condolences at a memorial service, you drink sugarless coffee. And when there is a conflict to solve, drinking coffee is the sign of reconciliation. I also learned that you never refuse coffee in someone's home. It is considered a major insult, as it's a symbol of relationship and hospitality.

A few years ago, my oldest brother, Mustafa, called me and said, "Come over now—I caught a burglar in my house." I arrived 15 minutes later to find about 100 family members gathered outside the house. My cousins were angry and demanded that my brother bring the burglar outside so they could "teach him a lesson." When my father arrived, he asked everyone to calm down. He then walked into the house to speak with the burglar. When my father eventually reemerged, he told everyone to let him go unharmed.

The burglar was 19 years old. He had broken into the house while my sister-in-law was out, hastily shoving a few valuables in a bag. But when she and the family returned, he was trapped; he hid and found himself locked in for the night (in the Middle East, windows often have bars, and steel doors are locked from the inside at night).

My brother Mustafa found the thief the next morning. He grabbed the teen, pushed him into a room, locked the door, and called all of us. When my father heard the story, he said, "I think we are lucky—we got the worst burglar in town." We all knew what my father was going to do. He was not going to call the police; he would resort to our traditional tribal conflict resolution method instead: a *sulha*.

He picked up his phone and called Abu Ayman, one of the elders of our tribe. Abu Ayman wears a Palestinian black and white *keffiyeh* (or scarf) and a traditional brown garment called an *abaya*. He commands respect in the whole country and is one of the most eloquent men I know. My father explained the situation to Abu Ayman, who arranged a meeting with the members of the thief's tribe.

The day of the council, more than a hundred men from my family convened. The youth among us wanted a show of strength and talked about revenge. Abu Ayman and the other elders listened and reasoned with us. The ultimate goal, they said, was to restore peace. Once we had decided on our demands, we elected Abu Ayman as our spokesperson and the representative of the family.

As soon as the tribal elders representing the thief's family arrived, we called for coffee to be served. As was tradition, the elders then declared they were there to solve the conflict and swore not to drink the coffee until we had reconciled.

The teen's family admitted that a crime had been committed, and they were willing to pay for that crime. They used an Arabic saying that translates to "Whatever you tailor for us, we will wear." Abu Ayman then laid down our demands: First, the teen (who had been high on drugs at the time of the break-in) needed to be put in a drug rehabilitation center. They agreed. Second, he would not be allowed in my brother's neighborhood for six months. They agreed. Finally, a financial payment would be owed to my brother for the social damages of disrespecting and breaching honor among neighbors. We started with $1 million. This was tradition: the offended tribe chooses a high number to show the severity of the crime committed.

The teen's tribal delegation agreed that it was a reasonable number, but they also knew that we were not expecting them to pay this amount. They thus countered with a traditional formula: "You are a generous and gracious people; you are people of faith. We ask for the sake of God that you bring that number down."

Abu Ayman responded, "For the sake of God, we will drop the number to half—only $500,000." The other family agreed again, and said, "For the sake of Prophet Muhammad, we ask your grace." Abu Ayman dropped the payment to $250,000 for the sake of the Prophet. Again, the family agreed. However, they continued, "For the sake of Jesus," and then later, "For the sake of Moses," and then for Abraham and other prophets and respected figures in our faith.

Within a few minutes, the $1 million became $20,000—an amount that everyone agreed upon. The delegation then asked for three days to collect the money. In our traditions, when one person commits a crime, it's the whole family who has to pay for it.

They finally lifted their untouched coffee on the table and began to drink—a sign that the reconciliation had been reached.

Three days later, the teen's family brought the money. My brother and I were excitedly planning what we would do with it. Go on vacation? Buy a car? Invest in a business? But before we had a chance to decide, my father interrupted us. "Don't waste your time; I'm giving the money back to them next week."

My brother and I were upset. "But this is our money!" we complained.

My father responded with a bit of wisdom: "We are a big family," he pointed out. The chances were good that one of us would do something stupid at some point. "If we are known as people who forgive, others will forgive us too. If we are known as people who take every penny we can, then others will have no mercy on us." Mustafa and I grudgingly accepted; we knew he was right.

"But then why did you take the money in the first place?" I asked. "You could have forgiven them right away. Why keep it for a few days?" My father explained that he wanted the family to feel consequences of what the thief had done. "I wanted them to take it seriously," he said. "By making each of them pay for his crime, everyone in the family is now involved, and will see to it that this young man gets the help he needs."

My father added that when he returned the money after a few days, the family would understand the meaning of the gesture more than if he had never taken the money at all.

This is how Palestinians (and many other Arabs) solve societal conflicts. And as travelers, there are many things we can learn from these practices. First and foremost is the importance of a cup of coffee: the gesture of sitting with another person and sharing a warm (or, in the case of the tribal council, cold) beverage. These moments of sitting and sharing life together, if you're willing to slow down and be present for them, can be infinitely more rewarding than Instagram pictures and checking off heritage sites from top-10 lists.

Second, the story illustrates the importance of listening to elders in the destinations we visit. Elders have unique, fascinating, and insightful knowledge, which can help make our world a kinder, more responsible place. They are the carriers of cultural traditions and can teach us about everything from different styles of conflict resolution to human relationships.

Finally, the story of the thief and the tribe speaks to the importance of grace and wisdom under pressure. As one travels around the world, things are bound to go awry, and people wrong me (intentionally and unintentionally) all the time. Sometimes it's the cranky, anxious, and tired people I'm traveling with; sometimes it's rude or racist hotel and restaurant staff. At other times, it's a pushy local, or a horde of loud and selfish tourists pushing their way around. But in these situations, it's important to remember: be gracious. You and I have been that rude person before (and sometime in the future, after a sleepless 10-hour flight, we will probably slip up and be that rude person again). But it's not all about me, my vacation, and what I want—it's about the betterment of all the communities involved in the travel experience. Stop. Breathe. Reflect. And act in ways that will make the world a more kind and humane place.

THE CASE FOR A DIFFERENT
KIND OF TRAVEL

Travel can be used to exacerbate cultural tensions, or it can be used to cross cultural divides. It can be used to build barriers or to cross boundaries. Travel can fuel xenophobia, prejudice, and social alienation, or it can be used to build a more peaceful world.

Travel has the potential to inspire us to become peacemakers in our everyday life. It introduces us to people we would not have met otherwise. It spurs us to reflect on ourselves and the decisions we make; it prompts us to reflect on our relationships with neighbors, friends, family members, and coworkers. I have seen people's lives completely change as a result of a trip, in which they were inspired to return home and apply what they had learned to their own lives.

I have seen people become more involved in their own communities. I witnessed a senior pastor who asked his church to revise his job description so that he could focus on fostering peace locally and internationally at his church and in his own community. He chose to be demoted from his senior pastor position to become a peacemaker working on local and international peacemaking projects. I have seen travelers go back home and reach out to different ethnic and religious communities in their own cities. I have seen groups organize to engage and help local organizations, entrepreneurs, women, and youth groups they met during their trips.

Travel can make us learn and appreciate the cultural differences we have with other communities. It provides opportunities to deal with conflicts, and to develop skills in problem-solving and peacemaking. Travel also gives us opportunities to learn about what others value, their communication style, and how they deal with and mitigate conflicts.

Finally, travel encourages us to explore the world's knowledge and wisdom. It can inspire us to stand up for what is right and can teach us to engage in peacemaking as ambassadors.

Rabbi Dr. Daniel Roth once told travelers in Israel and Palestine that they had the power and privilege to go almost anywhere in a country where most locals (Israelis and Palestinians alike) could not go, due to legal restrictions and because of fear and risk. Israelis don't go to Palestinian cities in the West Bank, and Palestinians don't go to Israeli cities. However, travelers can visit both places. They have the power to be the peacemakers of our country and help us connect with one another. Travelers, Dr. Roth told us, can and should be peacemakers.

So when you begin planning for your next trip—wherever that may be—ask yourself, "How can I be a peacemaker on my journey?" For I guarantee, you will always find ways to act as a peacemaker—even if it's just a small gesture to help someone in need, a kind word to service staff, or an extra measure of patience with fellow travelers.

In the end, travel is the opportunity of a lifetime. It is a chance for us to expand our minds and hearts, and engage with new ideas and perspectives—but only if we are mindful about how we travel.

NOTES

Chapter 1: Travel Is a State of Mind

1. "Fairfax County, VA," Data USA, accessed December 13, 2019, https://datausa.io/profile/geo/fairfax-county-va#about.

Chapter 2: The Case for (Responsible) Travel

1. Umair Irfan, "Air Travel Is Surging. That's a Huge Problem for the Climate," Vox, January 13, 2019, http://www.vox.com/energy-and -environment/2019/1/11/18177118/airlines-climate-change-emissions -travel.

2. WWF, "Tourists Cause Almost 40% Spike in Plastic Entering the Mediterranean Sea Each Summer," June 8, 2018, https://www .wwf.org.uk/updates/tourists-cause-almost-40-spike-plastic-entering -mediterranean-sea-each-summer.

3. World Travel and Tourism Council, "Tourism Supports 1 in 10 Jobs, Outpacing Global Economy for 6th Consecutive Year," March 20, 2017, https://www.wttc.org/about/media-centre/press-releases /press-releases/2017/tourism-supports-1-in-10-jobs-outpacing-global -economy-for-6th-consecutive-year-wttc/.

4. World Travel and Tourism Council, "Travel and Tourism Continues Strong Growth Above Global GDP," February 27, 2019, https:// www.wttc.org/about/media-centre/press-releases/press-releases/2019 /travel-tourism-continues-strong-growth-above-global-gdp/.

5. Elizabeth Becker, *Overbooked: The Exploding Business of Travel and Tourism* (New York: Simon & Schuster, 2016).

6. Marc von Lüpke-Schwarz, "A Brief History of Travel: From Elite Hobby to Mass Tourism," DW, August 4, 2013, https://www.dw.com /en/a-brief-history-of-travel-from-elite-hobby-to-mass-tourism /a-16996047.

7. Sinisa Jakov Marusic, Sven Milekic, and Dusica Tomovic, "Uncontrolled Tourism Threatens Balkan UNESCO Sites," Balkan Insight, April 17, 2017, https://balkaninsight.com/2017/04/17/uncontrolled-tourism-threatens-balkan-unesco-sites-04-13-2017/.

8. Jon Stone, "Dutch Tourist Board to Stop Promoting the Netherlands," *Independent*, May 7, 2019, https://www.independent.co.uk/travel/news-and-advice/netherlands-dutch-tourist-board-destination-city-amsterdam-tourism-a8903506.html.

9. Dov Lieber, "Israel Almost Entirely Halts Citizenship Approvals for East Jerusalemites," *Times of Israel*, September 26, 2016, https://www.timesofisrael.com/israel-almost-entirely-halts-citizenship-approvals-for-east-jerusalemites/.

10. Enric Sala, "Let's Turn the High Seas into the World's Largest Nature Reserve," TED2018, https://www.ted.com/talks/enric_sala_let_s_turn_the_high_seas_into_the_world_s_largest_nature_reserve/transcript?language=en.

11. Jo Griffin, "Why Tiny Belize Is a World Leader in Ocean Protection," *Guardian*, August 14, 2019, accessed November 1, 2019, https://www.theguardian.com/environment/2019/aug/14/why-tiny-belize-is-a-world-leader-in-ocean-protection.

12. Nick Clark, "Steven Hawking: Aggression Could Destroy Us," *Independent*, February 19, 2015, https://www.independent.co.uk/news/science/stephen-hawking-aggression-could-destroy-us-10057658.html.

13. Stephen Ryan, "Peace-Building and Conflict Transformation," in *Ethnic Conflict and International Relations* (Dartmouth, NH: Dartmouth Publishing, 1995), 131.

Chapter 3: What Does Responsible Travel Look Like?

1. "Responsible Tourism," Harold Goodwin: Taking Responsibility for Tourism, https://haroldgoodwin.info/responsible-tourism/.

2. From Sir R. Campbell, *Cairo: A document*, 1949, African Department—Egypt and Sudan, J 1319, Foreign Office Papers, National Archives, London, UK.

3. Sustaining Tourism, "Definitions," https://sustainabletourism .net/sustainable-tourism/definitions/.

4. Minority Rights Group International, "World Directory of Minorities: Afro-Colombians," https://www.justice.gov/sites/default /files/eoir/legacy/2014/02/19/Afro-Colombians.pdf.

5. Acotur, http://www.acotur.co.

6. Global Sustainable Tourism Council criteria, https://www.gst council.org/gstc-criteria. Global Sustainable Tourism Council, "GSTC Tour Operator Criteria, with Suggested Performance Indicators," Version 3, December 21, 2017, https://www.gstcouncil.org/wp-content /uploads/2015/11/GSTC-Tour-Operator_Industry_Criteria_with_tour _operator_indicators_21-Dec-2016_Final.pdf. Also see: Global Sustainable Tourism Council, "Criteria and Suggested Performance Indicators for Destinations," Version 1, December 10, 2013, https://www .gstcouncil.org/wp-content/uploads/2013/11/Dest-_CRITERIA_and _INDICATORS_6-9-14.pdf.

7. Travel industry B Corps and their ratings can be seen at https:// bcorporation.net/directory?search=&industry=Travel&Leisure.

8. LEED Rating System, US Green Building Council, https://www .usgbc.org/search?Search+Library=%22Hotels%22.

Chapter 4: Diversifying Your Itinerary

1. Shedia Invisible Tours, https://www.shedia.gr/tourguides/.

2. Diana Chigas, "Track II (Citizen) Diplomacy," Beyond Intractability, August 2003, https://www.beyondintractability.org/essaytrack2 -diplomacy.

Chapter 6: Avoiding "Voluntourism" and "Poverty Tourism"

1. Carrie Kahn, "As 'Voluntourism' Explodes in Popularity, Who's It Helping the Most?" *Morning Edition*, NPR, July 31, 2014, https://www.npr.org/sections/goatsandsoda/2014/07/31/336600290 /as-volunteerism-explodes-in-popularity-whos-it-helping-most.

2. Monica Pitrelli, "Orphanage Tourism: Help or Hindrance?" *Telegraph*, February 3, 2012, https://www.telegraph.co.uk/expat/expatlife/9055213/Orphanage-tourism-help-or-hindrance.html.

3. Christopher Knaus, "The Race to Rescue Cambodian Children from Orphanages Exploiting Them for Profit," *Guardian*, August 18, 2017, https://www.theguardian.com/world/2017/aug/19/the-race-to-rescue-cambodian-children-from-orphanages-exploiting-them-for-profit.

4. People and Places, https://travel-peopleandplaces.co.uk/.

5. "6-Day Visit to Rural African Village Completely Changes Woman's Facebook Profile Picture," *Onion*, January 28, 2014, https://www.theonion.com/6-day-visit-to-rural-african-village-completely-changes-1819576037.

Chapter 7: Overcoming Fear, Stereotypes, and Negativity

1. Anna Papadopoulos, "The World's Safest Cities Ranking, 2019," *CEOWorld Magazine*, August 1, 2019, https://ceoworld.biz/2019/08/01/the-worlds-safest-cities-ranking-2019/.

2. Just the Flight, "40 Tourist Scams to Avoid This Summer," https://www.justtheflight.co.uk/blog/16-40-tourist-scams-to-avoid-this-summer.html.

3. *USA Today*, "50 of the Most Dangerous Cities in the World," August 14, 2019, https://www.usatoday.com/picture-gallery/travel/news/2019/07/24most-dangerous-cities-world-tijuana-caracas-cape-town/1813211001/.

Chapter 9: A Woman's Perspective

1. Aditi Shrikant, "Women travel alone more than men. Here's why," Vox, January 18, 2019, https://www.vox.com/the-goods/2019/1/18/18188581/women-travel-alone-men.

2. Diane Daniel, "'Transformative Travel' Is the Industry's Latest Twist on Making Vacations More Meaningful," *Washington Post*, July

12, 2018, https://www.washingtonpost.com/lifestyle/travel/why-just
-go-on-vacation-when-you-can-have-a-life-changing-experience/2018
/07/11/a2886b6c-7eee-11e8-bb6b-c1cb691f1402_story.html.

3. Travel Aware, "Helping British Nationals Abroad 2015/16,"
Gov.uk, https://assets.publishing.service.gov.uk/government/uploads
/system/uploads/attachment_data/file/580501/161223_FCO_HBNA
_Report__Double_Pages_.pdf.

4. "Foreign Travel Advice: India," Gov.uk, https://www.gov.uk
/foreign-travel-advice/india.

Chapter 10: Fostering
Interreligious Exchange through Travel

1. Zenit staff, "Young Christians in Iraq Distribute Roses to
Muslims for Eid al Fitr Festival," Zenit, June 5, 2019, https://zenit.org
/articles/young-christians-in-iraq-distribute-roses-to-muslims-for-eid
-al-fitr-festival/.

Chapter 11: Revisiting Historical Narratives

1. Christopher Hibbert, *Redcoats and Rebels: The American Revolu-
tion Through British Eyes* (New York: W.W. Norton, 2002, reprint ed.).
Michael Pearson, *Those Damned Rebels: The American Revolution as Seen
Through British Eyes* (Boston, MA: Da Capo Press, 2000). Sami Adwan,
Dan Bar-On, and Eyal Naveh, eds., *Side by Side: Parallel Histories of
Israel-Palestine* (New York: The New Press, 2012).

Chapter 12: Resolving Conflict and
the Art of Responsible Travel

1. Certified B Corporation, B Corp Directory, https://bcorporation
.net/directory?search=&industry=Travel&Leisure.

2. "Rise in Unemployment in Palestine in 2018," Middle East
Monitor: Memo, April 30, 2019, https://www.middleeastmonitor.com
/20190430-rise-in-unemployment-in-palestine-in-2018/.

3. Kevin Avruch and Peter W. Black, "Conflict Resolution in Intercultural Settings," in *Conflict Resolution Theory and Practice: Integration and Application*, eds. Dennis J. D. Sandole and Hugo Van Der Merwe (Manchester, UK: Manchester University Press, 1993), 132.

4. Arno Michaelis, The Forgiveness Project, http://theforgiveness project.com/arno-michaelis.

ACKNOWLEDGMENTS

I AM VERY blessed to have an amazing group of friends who took the time to read the multiple drafts of the book and continuously helped me improve it. English is my second language, and I needed every one of you to point out idioms that don't work in English and grammar mistakes that I overlooked. Not only is this book better because of you, but my life is fuller because of your friendship.

I want to thank Scott H. Cooper, who has been my partner in building MEJDI Tours, our travel company. Scott's willingness to brainstorm and talk to me about every chapter of the book is appreciated. I am thankful for his patience as I took time off from work to finish the book.

I am full of gratitude to my friend Ellie Cleary for lending her unique perspective and insight to the book, and for believing in the project and in the role of tourism in creating a better world.

I am grateful to my editor Anna Leinberger, who has become a friend. Anna's support, willingness to talk anytime, and editing skills were so vital for the completion of this book.

I want to thank my team in MEJDI Tours for taking time to help me with the book. I asked them to read my drafts and help me with research. I want to thank Susan Jerzembski Holmer, who assisted me in making this book happen from inception to completion. This book would not have been completed without your support. This acknowledgment isn't complete without Kim Passy Yousef, Anne Bauer, Jazmin Avellaneda, and Seraphine, for their support in research, advice, and time.

I am thankful for the assistance of Dr. Harold Goodwin of World Travel Market Responsible Tourism, who was willing to give me advice and point me to the right resources. I am grateful to journalist Jaclynn Ashley, who spent many hours working with me and researching to make the first draft happen.

Most important, I am very grateful to Marie, my love, for believing in me, and continuing to inspire me and support me to write more, and for great feedback and substantial advice. Even as she was finishing her PhD dissertation, she was willing to take time off to help me with this project. I don't know what I could have done without her support.

INDEX

ABOUT THE AUTHOR

AZIZ ABU SARAH, recognized peace-builder, works around the globe as a cultural educator, mission-focused entrepreneur, and speaker. His journey, as a Palestinian raised in Jerusalem, from revenge to reconciliation has led him to cofound MEJDI Tours, a social enterprise focused on introducing multinarrative cultural education and responsible business practices to the travel industry. Honored as a National Geographic Explorer and TED Fellow for his conflict resolution and educational work throughout the world, he has written opinion pieces for the *New York Times*, the *Washington Post, National Geographic*, and CNN.

He served as executive director at the Center for World Religions, Diplomacy, and Conflict Resolution, George Mason University, and as a board member for the Parents Circle–Family Forum. Aziz is a recipient of the Goldberg Prize for Peace in the Middle East from the Institute of International Education, the Eliav-Sartawi Award for Middle Eastern Journalism, and the Intercultural Innovation Award from the United Nations Alliance of Civilizations and the BMW Group. He was named one of the World's 500 Most Influential Muslims by the Royal Islamic Strategic Studies Centre in Jordan. He was also recognized by UN Secretary General Ban Ki-moon for his work in peace building. Aziz Abu Sarah is changing the world, one trip at a time, as he aims to bring down the walls of intolerance and violence that plague our planet.

 MEJDI TOURS

ABOUT MEJDI TOURS

MEJDI Tours—the global leader in socially conscious travel— operates in more than 20 countries across five continents and is a Certified B Corporation.

MEJDI (MejdiTours.com) was founded by two peace-building experts, Aziz Abu Sarah and Scott Cooper. The unlikely duo of a Palestinian and an American Jew met each other while working on international development.

After becoming good friends and successfully designing social change programs all over the world, the pair discovered that travel was one of the most powerful and untapped resources for creating a better planet. They decided to take their unique experience and unmatched network of contacts to the travel sector.

MEJDI first gained accolades for creating the Dual Narrative™ in the Holy Land. This tour offered travelers the opportunity to have two tour guides (one Israeli and one Palestinian, guiding in tandem), each giving different historical, political, and cultural insights throughout the tour.

As MEJDI has expanded globally, its extremely diverse team has worked meticulously to implement and continuously refine the best approach of using travel as a vehicle for positive social change.

The results have been inspiring:

- They created global demand for Holy Land travel that features both Israelis and Palestinians.
- They have invested more than $15 million in local communities.
- They have supported more than 750 local nonprofits.

Berrett–Koehler
BK Publishers

Berrett-Koehler is an independent publisher dedicated to an ambitious mission: *Connecting people and ideas to create a world that works for all.*

Our publications span many formats, including print, digital, audio, and video. We also offer online resources, training, and gatherings. And we will continue expanding our products and services to advance our mission.

We believe that the solutions to the world's problems will come from all of us, working at all levels: in our society, in our organizations, and in our own lives. Our publications and resources offer pathways to creating a more just, equitable, and sustainable society. They help people make their organizations more humane, democratic, diverse, and effective (and we don't think there's any contradiction there). And they guide people in creating positive change in their own lives and aligning their personal practices with their aspirations for a better world.

And we strive to practice what we preach through what we call "The BK Way." At the core of this approach is *stewardship,* a deep sense of responsibility to administer the company for the benefit of all of our stakeholder groups, including authors, customers, employees, investors, service providers, sales partners, and the communities and environment around us. Everything we do is built around stewardship and our other core values of *quality, partnership, inclusion,* and *sustainability.*

This is why Berrett-Koehler is the first book publishing company to be both a B Corporation (a rigorous certification) and a benefit corporation (a for-profit legal status), which together require us to adhere to the highest standards for corporate, social, and environmental performance. And it is why we have instituted many pioneering practices (which you can learn about at www.bkconnection.com), including the Berrett-Koehler Constitution, the Bill of Rights and Responsibilities for BK Authors, and our unique Author Days.

We are grateful to our readers, authors, and other friends who are supporting our mission. We ask you to share with us examples of how BK publications and resources are making a difference in your lives, organizations, and communities at www.bkconnection.com/impact.

Dear reader,

Thank you for picking up this book and welcome to the worldwide BK community! You're joining a special group of people who have come together to create positive change in their lives, organizations, and communities.

What's BK all about?

Our mission is to connect people and ideas to create a world that works for all.

Why? Our communities, organizations, and lives get bogged down by old paradigms of self-interest, exclusion, hierarchy, and privilege. But we believe that can change. That's why we seek the leading experts on these challenges—and share their actionable ideas with you.

A welcome gift

To help you get started, we'd like to offer you a **free copy** of one of our bestselling ebooks:

www.bkconnection.com/welcome

When you claim your **free ebook**, you'll also be subscribed to our blog.

Our freshest insights

Access the best new tools and ideas for leaders at all levels on our blog at ideas.bkconnection.com.

Sincerely,

Your friends at Berrett-Koehler